Aging as a Shared Journey
A Guide for Healthy Aging

Monteen Lucas, PhD, CNS, RN

Health Positive! Inc.

Lawrence, KS, USA

Aging as a Shared Journey

This book is available at quantity discounts for bulk purchases for sales, promotions, fund-raising and educational needs. For details, telephone Monteen Lucas, PhD. at Eduplace: 1-785-840-0358 or send email to: eduplace@cjnetworks.com

Health Positive!, Inc.
1510 E. 1584 Road
Lawrence, KS 66046
1-785-843-5884
sharon@healthpositive.com

ISBN 0-9658690-1-6

Cover design & illustration by Sherri Treadwell.
Printed in the United States of America.
10 9 8 7 6 5 4 3 2 1

This book is dedicated to
My father, who believed
I could do anything
and
My daughters, who support me
in everything I do.

Aging as a Shared Journey

Contents

Prologue 13

Introduction and Overview 23

Chapter 1: Heartwork 41

Chapter 2: Relating Adult to Adult & Learning to
Use RISC 67

Risking Changes in the Parent - Adult Child Relationship .. 73
Risking Changes in Other Adult Relationships 81
Learning to Use the RISC Strategy to Improve Adult - Adult
Relationships 86

Chapter 3: Meeting the Challenges of Aging & Illness ... 99

Aging and Ageism 102
The Adult-to-Adult Focus and the Caregiver Relationship 105
Applying the RISC Strategy to Adapting to Illness and Disability . 109
Depression 116
Common Responses to Illness and Disability 120
Climate of Acceptance 128

Chapter 4: Communicating Clearly & Compassionately .. 131

Guidelines for Improving Communication 133
Stress Reduction and Communication 137
Adult-to-Adult Communication Between Younger and Older
People 140
Overcoming Barriers to Compassionate Communication 144
Communication Skills Needed For Working Through RISC 148
Communication Exercises to Build Your Skills for the Journey . 153

Chapter 5: Resolving Unfinished Business 161

Chapter 6: Facing The End of the Journey 185

Epilogue: A Fable 213

Appendix for Mental Health Professionals 217

References 243

Index 255

Aging as a Shared Journey

About the Author

Monteen Lucas, Ph.D., CNS, R.N. is a national leader in psychogeriatric nursing, a specialty devoted to the mental health and psychiatric needs of elders. She has spent 25 years in advanced practice as a Clinical Nurse Specialist and a psychotherapist. In 1975, she received her dual Masters degree in Psychiatric-Mental Health Nursing and in Community Health Nursing from Texas Woman's University. Dr. Lucas' Ph.D. in Health Education and Administration from Texas A&M University (1987) was accompanied by her Certification from Baylor College of Medicine for completion of graduate studies in Allied Health Education and Administration.

In her lengthy career as educator and clinician, Dr. Lucas has practiced in university settings and in the community, homes, hospitals and clinics as well as private practice in individual, group, and family therapy. In 1997, she resigned her position at Yale University School of Nursing as Associate Professor and Coordinator of Psychogeriatric-Mental Health Nursing. In conjunction with her faculty appointment, she held a joint appointment to Yale-New Haven Hospital as Psychogeriatric-Mental Health Consultation-Liaison Nurse Specialist. Since relocating to Lawrence, Kansas in 1997, she has re-opened EDUPLACE, the consulting and education business she operated in Houston, Texas in the 1980's.

The author has worked with elders and their families in community groups in Houston and New Haven and in private therapy. She pioneered mental health services for the elderly in the 1970's in Houston, Texas, where she designed and directed a geriatric mental health center that was on the 'cutting edge' of its time. Her Masters thesis was based on her research at the center, where she studied behavioral interventions to improve the mental health of elders. Her findings demonstrated elders' ability to change in positive ways when they developed healthy relationships and received support through transitions. She has continued to build on those early findings as she developed the guide for healthy aging upon which this book is based. Her work with mental health professionals includes workshops to teach the use of her model for healthy aging as a clinical intervention.

Among her professional associations, she is a member of the International Federation on Ageing, the American Society on Aging, the Mental Health and Aging Network, the American Psychiatric Nursing Association, the Mid-America Congress on Aging, and Sigma Theta Tau International, the nursing honor society. She was the recipient of the first Nurse Educator Award presented by the International Psychiatric-Consultation-Liaison Nurses Society. She was a founding member of the American Holistic Nursing Association.

Dr. Lucas' work is on the forefront of the burgeoning awareness of the need for new paradigms for intergenerational adult relationships. A lifelong challenger of stereotypes, she began working with her newspaper editor father in his newspaper and printing business at age 10. By the time she entered Emory University in Atlanta, Georgia, at age 16, she had experience in writing, proofreading, typesetting, publicity, and customer relationships in small towns throughout the south.

As a dedicated 'maverick' she remains as true as possible to the promise she made to Maggie Kuhn, founder of the Grey Panthers, to "do something outrageous" every day. One of her daughters created the art work for the cover of this book. Her other daughter helped create her seven grandchildren. A champion of healthy intergenerational living, she maintains friendships with people of many different ages and is a staunch supporter of intergenerational community involvement. When people ask her when she plans to retire, she answers, "The date of my death has not been determined."

Among her goals for the future, Dr. Lucas intends to disseminate her model through workshops, writing, and speaking, to pursue her interests in drama, storytelling, and humor as facilitators of mental health, to open her heart to an increasing circle of family and friends, and to enrich her spiritual life for the remaining minutes, hours, or days of her life. Then she expects to move to adventures beyond this realm

In Gratitude

Gratitude – such a good word to describe my overwhelming feelings of thankfulness to a large contingent of people who enrich my life. First, I am grateful there are too many to list. I wrote a long list for an 'Acknowledgments' section and was overcome with such wonder at the length, diversity and quality of the people on it that I couldn't finish it. I decided that what I have to 'acknowledge' is the inadequacy of my effort to do justice to those people. For them, what I have is gratitude.

... for my father, grandmother, and brother who loved me unconditionally, protected me, challenged me, and helped me grow up in a difficult environment

... for my teachers who supported me, challenged me, and showed me I could learn to speak up for myself with my peers

... for my daughters and grandchildren

... for the family and friends who make up my closest 'inner circle' – the ones I call my stardust companions. Their innumerable contributions to my life and health would fill a book much larger than this one

... for my students who trusted me, challenged me, and helped me learn what it means to understand that the teacher teaches what she needs to learn

... for my colleagues who share my vision and for those who do not. The former help me dream and grow. The latter help me keep the vital importance of my vision sharpened.

... for those who have become both friends and colleagues as we have shared personal, emotional, spiritual, and professional development through the years

... for the authors of the books I 'lived' in for my first 16 years, and for those I continue to live with - some old, some new

... for the many clients, strangers, friends and others who encouraged me to write about how I was practicing in life and as a professional – some are quoted on the cover

... for the people in the publishing business who told me no one would read my book, thus ensuring I would write it

... and for Sharon, whose encouragement, knowledge, and dedication to task so beautifully embodies the 'midwife' analogy she used in making this dream a reality.

Prologue

"Aging as a Shared Journey" is about exploring...exploring within oneself...exploring within relationships. Thinking about people my age traveling to places everyone "should" see before they die, I become deeply introspective. It seems like a good idea to see new places in my country and to see other countries before I die, even to revisit favorite places from past years. Nonetheless, I wonder whether the authentic 'me' will be changed by those places.

I ponder what inner changes would be prerequisite to being shaped, formed, and stretched by traveling to those places. Kabat-Zinn seems to have expressed it best: "wherever you go there you are." (Kabat-Zinn, J., 1994).

I look closely at the faces and study the body language of elderly people sitting in senior centers, walking along sidewalks, gathering in communal areas of assisted living homes, lying in beds in nursing homes. I pay particular attention to studying those who are in my Tai Chi class for beginners, persons queued up for the bus to tour the state capitol, others pursuing 'the good life' after the birthday with the magic number, 65. I am acutely aware they brought themselves and much of their old life baggage with them on the trip.

I notice I especially want to distance myself from those who are so painstakingly 'made up' to look like ads in magazines...the stylish '30-something' clothing and young hairdos thinly disguising the pain of aging. I sit or stand with these elderly people and go deep within myself, searching out my authentic responses to my experiences. "I hate this" echoes through my being.

Like my 3-year old grandson says when told he should be somewhere he does not want to be: "I don't want me there!" Now, there is an authentic response to which I can feel every fiber of my being resonate – "I DON'T WANT ME HERE!"

I am musing about the last time I settled into pure joy and contentment about "being here." I was in my little home in Trinity, studying A Course In Miracles, nestling into my wooded surroundings, relaxing in the hot tub overlooking the lake, completing my dissertation, chuckling about the people who worried that I didn't know where I wanted to be next.

"Stars and Hearts" meditation from my journal.

...settled into the nurturing evening with Edens'
The Starcleaner Reunion. It warms my heart to pore
over it again...to reminisce about the talks Sherri
and I had about star-cleaners and stardust compan-
ions. The stars in the book are lonely until they are
polished and gathered – so they can shine and be
together in a 'home.' Their home keeps bursting and
becoming bigger, because it is too small to contain

the happiness generated by their shared joy. This
wonderful fable ends with the stars becoming our
own hearts – "the stars' joy had become so great that
they had no place greater to be."

For months now, I have meditated and prayed
and talked about the nature of relationships with
people with whom we share our hopes and dreams.
The loneliness of past losses and present absences
recedes as I pursue my dreams with others who
risk going after their own. The pangs of past hurts
and regrets diminish as I share my light with others
who are 'lit from within.' Sherri found a perfect
card that I keep with my treasures. "It is never easy
to keep reaching for dreams. Strength and courage
can sometimes be lonely friends...but those who
reach walk in stardust." (Flavia). We vowed to be
stardust companions as we live out our lives, as we
share the journey.

Sometimes the journey will be deep and even
painful. Sometimes it will be superficial and somewhat like a farce. At times, it will be funny, joyful,
and bittersweet. Sometimes it will bring up shame,
embarrassment, or anger. It will have moments of
satisfaction for past accomplishments as well as
moments of disappointment for past failures.

To remain grounded – and to explore this relatively unknown terrain – I will remind myself that
God and my stardust companions are here with me.
I will remind myself that the determination to do
this is a risk; but it is also a choice. YES, I am taking a different trip. I am going exploring inside ME
to the territory that has been unrecognized ...
repressed ... controlled ... shut down ... shut up ...
scared to come out.

I want to poke around deep inside to and through the peaks and valleys and caves inside myself – way down into territory I call my soul. I vow to report what I find there as clearly and as honestly as I can. It will take time...it will change as I become more familiar with the terrain...it will, I pray, be still in process when I draw my last breath. But here goes!

The pattern of exploration repeats itself over and over again as I move in different realms of my life experience: my soul-self; my mother-self; my friend-self; my professional-self; my healer-self; my wife-self; my lover-self; my wisdom-woman self; my warrior-self; and the selves I discover and uncover along the way. I pray for guidance, meditate until I am grounded and centered, and dive in.

I cannot stay indefinitely within the solitary realm inside me but plunge in like a swimmer going to the bottom of the sea and surface for air when I can hold my breath no longer. Surfacing, I draw sustenance from those with whom I am in relationship – my loved ones – and especially those who know me from inside my own skin and whom I call my stardust companions. From my journal:

> *The fear is like an inner lining of ice that coats my insides...when I feel filled with joy and grace, I don't notice it...too much warmth and too light-filled to even remember my ice-lining. I was born with this fear...she was afraid to have me, and I was afraid to be born to her. My intellect has at last stopped trying to convince me this will not be part of me for my lifetime. I intellectualize well, though the effect is only temporary, of course. I call up thoughts like*

"the cells that line my insides have been replaced
hundreds of times through these many years." True.
Equally true that they always find living in there ice
cold, because the fear that chills them was pre-"me."
It was formed inside her, so it could not have been
otherwise. Fear was what she was made of – how
terrified she was as she dedicated her life to terrifying me.

Layers of loving and being loved, of learning and
accomplishing, of knowing God's grace, of a life filled
with living have kept me warm much of the time.
Settling into my warmth, I can consciously forget
the ice-lining. Years in which I convinced myself it
had melted – years of making love, playing with my
babies, watching my daughters grow, becoming
successful in my career, forging deep and abiding
friendships, developing various versions of my
philosophy of life. Those years interspersed with
occasional interruptions. ONE JOLT strong enough
to displace the warmth and there it is – the ice-lining
– just waiting; being there, to touch me with the
chill so piercing it can penetrate anything.

I go to classes and teach my students about growth
and development, about maturity, about individuat-
ing and re-inventing the self one truly wishes to be.
And I work harder than anyone at being the example
– and at proving it can be done. Each time the ice-
lining breaks through to my awareness, I must work
hard to re-gather enough warmth layers to snuggle
in again and repair and re-grow myself, with God's
help. "Do your inner child work" the part-people,
part automaton therapy mimics chant. How insuffi-
cient such "canned" approaches!

Of course, it helps some, sort of a 'band-aid' for the
pain. Nonetheless, when I am "inside myself"
frantically gathering back the layers of warmth to
keep from freezing with the fear, I know at the primal

level of survival that if I do not do my soul-work, I am extinguished.

I get warm again, and I go exploring round my soul...it's not geographical...it's not anatomical ...my soul is inside/outside 'me.' Soul knows no fear; has only one perception some might label emotion: LOVE. Despite the formless nature of my soul, I can delve into it; wander around in it; describe it – not fully, but enough to grasp something of its essence.

...long stretches of peaceful green space; soft like velvet; restful; safe...

...sky blue atmosphere in which I float weightlessly; serene; safe...

...light-filled something in which I bask in the warmth and penetration of the healing light...safe

...bubbles all around; I bounce within the bubbles; float with them; feel joyous...safe...

...expanding; feeling wonder; no need to control...just 'is-ness;' full and free...light as a breeze...wafting around in no particular direction...loving...safe

...no sense of time...is this eternity?

There it is, my old familiar intellect, wanting to label my experiences. I feel it pulling me away from my reverie, my soul-exploring. It's like a tether that jerks me back from the soul wonder, awe, joy, love. But wait! If I am *in* my soul I cannot be jerked out of it, so what happens?

Perhaps my intellect needs to explore my soul in a different mode. Why would that be? The pure perception, pure feeling is so vivid, so real. It should be enough. LOOK OUT! The 'shoulds' have entered; the intellect is on guard.

I'm back in alert mode. What shifted? Awareness of the clock ticking, for one thing. Remembering I am supposed to be some place where I promised to meet someone. Wondering why I needed to skip into alert mode to go on with the day. I put on my clothes and my ego armor and surface, desperately trying to remember I need to touch someone – to be more real by being with someone – like the Velveteen Rabbit, I become "real" only in relationship (Williams, M., 1975).

I sit and talk with people superficially about local news, last night's television fare, grandchildren, the weather. I think, "how might this conversation develop if we felt free to talk about our inner selves?" That kind of talk is risky; "...if I tell you who I am, you may not like who I am, and it is all that I have" (Powell, J. 1969). This is not only my wish to be known for my real self, but also to know the other – to develop deep, meaningful and abiding relationships in and through which I can make this strange journey into the unfamiliar territory of 'aging' with people I trust.

I yearn to share the journey with those who are my companions on the journey. We can help one another find our way. Together, we can discover ways to deal creatively with the difficulties of our passages. We can find ways to uncover joys, exciting surprises, fulfillment, and discoveries as we age. If we do that, we will be safe enough with one another, in loving relationships, to help one another prepare for the journey's end, death.

With strong bonds forged through traveling together as pioneers in the terrain of aging, we can help one another usher in the beginnings that follow the death of life as we now know it.

How can I interest anyone in taking such a journey with me? Perhaps if I were able to paint a picture of the terrain that gives them a better idea of what it might be like to come along. Travel posters entice us to buy tickets to fly to exotic places, to take ski lifts and helicopter rides over vast territory to obtain a 'bird's eye' view. Something like that – a picture that captures the look, feel, colors, hues, textures one could encounter along the way.

Once some of us encounter the terrain as fellow journeyers, then surely some of us will become poets who can paint such pictures with words, artists who can put them on canvas, musicians who can set the strange, unfamiliar sounds to music, and writers who can write guide-books complete with maps. What would those sights, sounds, words look like if they captured fleeting glimpses of the soul?

The quality of light is as elusive to description as the quality of my inner being when I want to describe it in minute detail that captures every nuance;

play of shadows; wisps of form that melts into the formless; filtered light that is translucent;

fading light that gives way to the illusion of black until the eyes adjust and tones and hues can be discerned;

feeling the deep conviction tumbling around inside me that I must search for words that can serve as

*transport to let my heart express itself from the
inside;*

*yearning to connect with others in relationship at the
deep, soul level ... connect with the Heart of the
Universe;*

*strong, durable form that undergirds and supports
my being as it dances; flows; changes hues and
qualities as it "plays" with the light – healing light –
as in a breeze.*

If I find ways to create words that transport and convey my soul perspective, will they speak to anyone else? Will they be simply idiosyncratic 'mutterings?' I think not. I believe that if whatever is the outcome of this search comes truly from my heart, then it will speak to other hearts. It is a work somewhat akin to harvesting my soul so that it can be poured out to help nourish others.

The result comes after working on the developmental "task" of the last stage of life (Erikson, E.H., Erikson, J.M., & Kivnick, H.Q., 1986) with hundreds of people, and now myself. It emerges out of the context of what it means to be an 'elder,' the unfinished business of "what is important that I do before I die?" and my need to meld my own lived experience with what I have learned from others on the journey.

Enjoy the journey! May it speak deeply to your heart and soul!

*the fear slips back inside, the ice-lining, threatening
to destroy me...but it will not...my inner resilience
will push it back and my loving relationships will*

*create the warm space to curl up into...of course, it's
a risk...my old companion, risk, gradually turns into
a cozy, comfortable feeling like an old, worn, loved
robe...I'm learning to love 'old'...and I am not
alone...I will, again and again, take the risk...*

"Monteen, promise me you'll do something outrageous
every day for the rest of your life."
Maggie Kuhn

Introduction and Overview

"Life is either a daring adventure or nothing."
Helen Keller

Introduction

Approaching aging and illness with a mentally healthy attitude requires a balanced perspective. In fact, 'maintain a balanced perspective' could serve as the 'banner' for this book! We see the bombardment of health claims that assail the public about aging virtually everywhere — television, magazines, newspapers, internet, and radio. Public media resources, organizations devoted to aging, and even research reports hold conflicting 'messages' about aging. Accurate, well-balanced information about the process of aging can be difficult to distinguish from 'hype.' On one hand we hear, "aging has been conquered!" On the other extreme, we are exhorted to "prepare yourself financially to end up in a long-term care facility." Clearly, it is pivotal to begin our look into the journey of aging by affirming the importance of a balanced perspective.

The public is awakening to the impact of staggering demographics. Members of the 'baby boomer' generation have begun to celebrate their fiftieth birthdays. In the United States alone, one in six people will be over 65 by the year 2020. Of those, approximately 6.5 million will be over the age of 85. Currently, 60% of the world's population over age 60 are in developing countries. By the year 2020, that figure is expected to rise to 70%. Older women outnumber men the world over by a ratio of 2:1. Ken Dychtwald calls it the "age wave," and aging is IN.

Having studied the field of aging since 1974, I assure you there is both cause for hope and cause for caution. The hopeful research indicates, for example, that memory loss is not inevitable as we age. The value of a healthy lifestyle to improving the quality of life gets a lot of attention, but so does Dr. Kevorkian! Some stereotypes persist that have been with us for generations. Outdated prejudices remain despite new findings about development throughout the lifespan. Mistaken beliefs that contribute to prejudice against older people reflect what Robert Butler termed, "ageism."

Ageism remains prevalent among older people as well as their families, health care providers, and the general population. It is difficult to keep pace with findings that challenge old ideas, old 'facts' about aging. Data pour in from many fields, such as neurology (e.g., brain research), cell biology, pharmacology, genetics, nutrition, behavioral and social sciences, gerontology, prevention and wellness interests, on and on. In the midst of the hodgepodge of new vs. old, fact vs. myth, and hope vs. hype, it is wise to keep our perspective on an even keel.

In an effort to bring a balanced perspective to my practice as a Clinical Nurse Specialist and Nurse Psychotherapist, I began developing this guide for "Aging as a Shared Journey" in 1988. The pattern for the guide is derived from qualitative data related to my practice. The methodology is presented in more detail in the Appendix for readers who wish to know more about it from an academic perspective. The applicability of this guide for healthy aging is virtually universal, as we are entering the most expansive era of multigenerational families in history.

Today's 'boomers' are looking at their potential for living longer than ever before. Some of them look at old people and wonder, as Robert Butler wrote nearly 30 years ago, " why survive growing old...?" They ask themselves, "If my quality of life cannot be better than what I see in nursing homes; in the stooped, shuffling gait of old people on the street; in the vacant stares and looks of resignation on the faces of old folks languidly pushing dominoes in a Senior Center, why indeed?"

Today, more than ever before, adult children are aware of aging – not only in their parents, but of their own aging. Today's adult children and their parents are likely to have years, even decades, of relatively good health. During those years, they can be helped to release outmoded roles and establish a new sense of connection. Becoming connected in an adult-to-adult context can enable each of them to feel valued, nurtured, and accepted as they respond to the challenges of aging. Aging is a developmental process. It is never too early to begin living healthier lives and developing mentally healthier attitudes about aging. And, as Sarah L.

Delaney said at age 107, "we are never too old to change!"

I use personal pronouns throughout the book in order to communicate the interpersonal messages from me to you just as I deliver them when I teach this guide to people individually and/or in workshops. Generally speaking, when I address "you," I am addressing those adults who are in close relationship with persons 65 or over. I expect that you had one or more older adult relationships in mind when you picked up this book. You are likely to be the adult child of elder parents, and the demographics indicate that you are most likely to be a 'boomer.' I refer to the parents, spouses, and friends in your life who are over 65 years old as "elders."

Researchers and others who study aging and common illnesses in the aging population typically define old persons as those 65 and over. Strictly speaking, the use of age 65 or over was derived from applying social norms of age of retirement, social security, and other such standards to determining old age. That arbitrary gateway into old age may continue to be accepted by our culture a few more years; but it will break down as you 'boomers' approach that age!

When I speak about those 65 and over in the third person, I use the term 'elders' because it connotes more positive associations with the knowledge, wisdom, and stature that age and experience can bring. When I am addressing my comments directly to elders, I have made a conscientious effort to make that clear. The personal pronoun "we" denotes all of us – adults of any age –

and I have used it from time to time to emphasize the intergenerational nature of aging.

This book is about learning to recognize the need for change – at any age. It is about managing change successfully through the use of a specific approach. To name the approach I used an acronym, **RISC**. The acronym stands for the steps involved in using it:
  1) **R**ecognizing
  2) **I**nventorying
  3) **S**tructuring and
  4) **C**hoosing

RISC is described in the section below about the design of the guide. As you consider how the guide is designed, it will be helpful to think of each different part, for example, relating adult-to-adult, as one of the parts of the territory of aging we are exploring on our journey.

My practice consists of decades of helping people learn how to respond to the changes they want in their lives, how to make them, or how to 'live well' when certain things could not be changed. As those efforts focused increasingly on older people, I began to use the term 'aging well' to refer to healthy aging. Each year the number of people discovering how vital it is to age well is growing.

Many of us, by the time we reach our middle years of life, find ourselves feeling locked into recurring interactions with our parents, another relative, a spouse, or a friend – that are repetitive, predictable, boring, or even distressing. When patterns like these recur, we stop listening to one

another and too often sink into ruts of resignation
- "so this is what becoming old is like?"

Instead of being open to options to change and
open to the other, we 'steel' ourselves in order to
defend against our feelings of boredom, anger,
anxiety, or frustration. People who describe themselves as being "in a mid-life crisis" give descriptions of such interactions to their therapists. I have
heard years of such comments from my clients.
Comments such as, "I know exactly what he's going
to say when I say 'Mom invited us for dinner.' He
will get that bored look on his face and say, 'and
you're going to tell me why we have to go.'" When
her adult daughter says, "I know you and I disagree
on this, but..." her mother might think, "Here we
go again."

Think about your own life. How many descriptions could you give of times when you feel locked
into old patterns of reacting? In this book, I use
dynamic vignettes from my own experience to
demonstrate how the use of the guide and the **RISC**
strategy can give you the means to move from
feeling trapped and bogged down to being more in
charge and freer in relationships.

We do not have a 'road map' for this unprec-
edented journey. One thing is certain: how we
make our journey into aging will make a difference.
The journey can be a continuation of our growth
and development. This guide points the way. You
and I are pioneers who are making our journey into
territory virtually unknown. We must chart our
course as we go, like the true explorers we are.

Each chapter of the book will provide you with some practical information about the territory you are exploring. The case vignettes will show you how pioneers who came before you used the guide. Each experience you share with your elders will help them on their journey. Each experience you share with your peers will help them with their elders.

We cannot know precisely what we will find in each moment of our journey, but we can choose to use what has been learned by fellow explorers to help us live vital lives to journey's end. George Burns was fond of saying he did not plan to die: "It's been tried; there must be another way."

In my case, and in the midst of different beliefs about aging, I plan to die. I plan to do it well; and in the meantime, I plan to live well. I expect my parting thoughts regarding the multitude of beliefs about aging will be something like, "I'm still on the edge of my seat...waiting to see how it turns out!" I want to add the voice of my own experience to the world's view of aging and to add some spice to it! Yes, that is the core of my guide – Choosing to age with others, in the spirit of shared adventure!

Overview

Basic Assumptions

This guide for healthy aging was developed using specific statements that serve as the foundation for a statement of belief about "Aging as a Shared Journey." The primary understanding is this: aging and the changing balance of dependence/independence require new approaches to relating to others and to our communities as adults. Within our families, both adults – children and parents – are aging; but at any age, a parent is still a parent. The same premise applies to spouses and other adults in relationship. An adult remains an adult despite changes related to illness or disability associated with aging. Aging well requires learning new ways of relating that are congruent with maintaining our identities as adults.

The basic assumptions that support the underlying statement of belief are:

1. At any age, your parent is still your parent. The roles you and your parents take may change over time, but reversing roles denigrates the value of your parent/child bond.

2. Aging and the changing balance of dependence/independence require new approaches to relating to one another as adults.

3. Both adults in a relationship are aging; you and your parents, you and your spouse, friend, child, partner, or any other adult with whom you are connected closely.

4. Changes in functional status that may occur in association with illness and/or disability as people age are not synonymous with similarities in emotional, psychological, or spiritual development. For example, an adult with weakened sphincter control who wears protective undergarments is still an adult - not an infant in 'diapers'

5. The possibilities for continuing enrichment of friendships, parent/child relationships,

and for building community as you age provide you and other adults with whom you relate with 'win-win' situations.

6. The adults of today who choose to undertake this journey into aging in collaboration with others and in the spirit of shared adventuring are the pioneers whose explorations, discoveries, and insights (as well as errors) will inform and light the way to healthier ways of living until we die.

The methodology used to 'build' my guide is discussed in more detail in the Appendix for Mental Health Professionals. A brief summary of the theories that were most influential in constructing the work follows.

Erik Erikson's theory of psychological growth throughout the life cycle delineates eight stages of development from birth to death. They are: 1) Basic Trust vs. Basic Mistrust 2) Autonomy vs. Shame and Doubt 3) Initiative vs. Guilt 4) Industry vs. Inferiority 5) Identity vs. Confusion 6) Intimacy vs. Isolation 7) Generativity vs. Stagnation and 8) Integrity vs. Despair. The name of each stage corresponds with a major developmental task that characterizes that stage.

Mastery of each task marks healthy development, and incomplete mastery of each task is described as its antithesis. For example, if you are a middle-aged adult, your primary task is generativity, which is manifested by caring for your family and community. The ability to CARE effectively is the outcome of successful mastery of this stage of development. Inadequate mastery of generativity results in stagnation, often manifest as self-absorption. The stages are not self-contained, but they flow into one another.

As we grow and develop we find ourselves working through them in different ways appropriate to the context of our lives. For example, the infant who masters the first stage and develops basic trust will grow toward further development of that task when faced with future stages such as developing stronger identity and mastering intimacy vs. isolation.

My findings indicate that many conflicts between adult children and their parents are rooted in conflicts between the child's demanding task of generativity vs. self-absorption and the parent's need to master the equally demanding task of the last stage of development, integrity vs. despair.

Resolving the tension inherent in mastering integrity vs. despair challenges the individual to rework the tensions and rebalance the strengths of all earlier stages. By doing the reworking and re-balancing, the elder attempts to "establish an integrity of the self" that both draws sustenance from the past and remains vitally involved in the present. (Erikson, et al, 1986). To accomplish this daunting feat, parents – whether or not they voice it – want their children to understand what they are going through.

On the other hand, you as a mid-life adult, are in a more powerful phase of life. Erikson described your task, generativity vs. stagnation, as 'taking care of' institutions, professions, and families. He stressed that the world is in your hands. It is no wonder volumes have been written about 'caregiver burden.' Perhaps in paying more attention to the burden of being the ones taking care of the world, we need to learn ways for both generations to work together in partnership to take care of the world.

Being in different stages, confronted with different life tasks can create a gulf between generations. There is, however, another choice – collaborating as sojourners. In my experience working with this approach, I find generations able to support one another if they release outmoded roles and establish a sense of connection within an appropriate adult-to-adult context.

Another theory upon which the work strongly relies is the Interpersonal Relationships theory as developed by Hildegard Peplau, who demonstrated the power of establishing a therapeutic alliance with patients. A therapeutic alliance is one in which both parties are committed to growth toward healthier relationship through effective communication and better understanding of the other. Such an alliance between the persons in relationship provides an environment in which healthy change can occur, resulting in healthier behavior.

Having begun using the therapeutic alliance as a means of establishing healthy boundaries between myself and my patients, I learned that such relationships are equally effective in promoting healthier interpersonal environments in families and among other adult relationships. Therefore, Peplau's concepts are integrated into teaching how to use the guide to share the journey.

Carl Rogers observed that life is, at its best, a process in which nothing is fixed but rather life flows and changes. His words are almost literally descriptive of this journey. Rogers' concept of "unconditional positive regard" helps elucidate what is meant by the climate of acceptance within which those who undertake the journey do their work. Preparation for creating a 'climate of acceptance' begins with doing what I call one's 'heartwork'. The issues involved in heartwork are discussed in Chapter 1 and threaded throughout the book.

You may be using the book along with an elder or an adult peer who chooses to study it and practice it with you. If you are reading it alone, think about the significant elders in your life as you do the exercises, apply the suggestions, and do your heartwork. The heartwork is different for each unique individual, yet I find common threads of experience among the people whom I teach to use this guide for healthy aging.

The case vignettes chosen to illustrate various applications of this approach may sound familiar to you in some way. You may be reminded of people you know and situations you have experienced, or find other commonalities with your fellow travelers on the journey as you read and work with the guide.

In various ways, my work with elders demonstrated the value of learning from them what is meaningful in their lives. Many of their decisions, their willingness to attempt change, and their quality of life are influenced by what Mary Baird Carlsen called "meaning-making." I relied strongly on Carlsen's developmental theory that builds the foundation for her work with meaning-making as I developed the guide.

Design of the Guide

There are five basic parts that make up the pattern of the journey – or, in other words, the design of the guide:
1) Relating Adult to Adult
2) Meeting the Challenges of Aging and Illness
3) Communicating Clearly and Compassionately
4) Resolving Unfinished Business
5) Facing the End of the Journey.

The order in which each section is addressed may depend on variables in the specific relationship of the adults involved. In the workshop format, the sections are presented in the order shown in the book. The **RISC** strategy is incorporated into each of the parts of the design. In the book, it is presented in detail in Chapter 2, "Relating Adult to Adult."

Each part is discussed in subsequent chapters accompanied by instructions in the use of pertinent strategies and case vignettes for mastery of the material. Case vignettes were developed to illustrate various applications of the guide to health assessment, psychotherapy, therapeutic alliance with families, and teaching and counseling parents and adult children. The vignettes were edited to protect the confidentiality of the clients on whose experiences they are based.

As you work through the journey using the strategies and vignettes along with exercises and suggestions to stimulate thoughts and feelings

about your own life experiences, you can develop
an increasing awareness of how each part is related
to all the others. A brief description of each section follows.

Relating Adult to Adult

Communication exercises, relaxation exercises,
role-play, and other experiential learning strategies
are utilized to teach participants how to:

a) respect their differences

b)   negotiate as equals while mindful of parent - adult child relationship

c) negotiate as equals while mindful of spousal
or other adult relationships

d) learn new ways to talk, work, and play together

e) allow space for growth separately and together

f) move the balance of dependence/indepen-
dence toward interdependence in their relationship

Learning to Use **RISC**

There are risks in letting your parent, your
adult child, your spouse, and/or your friends know
who you really are. Participants are helped to do
an assessment of their readiness to take risks
within the context of recognizing that not taking
risks is a risk in itself. They are taught an ordered
approach for which the acronym **RISC** was coined
for use in this guide.

The **RISC** strategy involves four steps: 1) Recognizing, 2) Inventorying, 3) Structuring and 4)
Choosing. A significant portion of workshop time
is devoted to teaching and practicing the use of
RISC. Communication, stress reduction, and other
skills are threaded through all of the work. The

steps of the process are used to work on tasks related to each of the specific parts, or sections, of the journey, for example, death and dying.

Meeting the Challenges of Aging and Illness
Beginning with a discussion of the climate of acceptance as the context within which the journey must take place, participants are helped to explore the following:
a) decisions about health they currently face as well as those they anticipate
b) decisions about financial and legal concerns (referrals to legal and financial resources for advice)
c) independence/dependence issues
d) decisions about how and where to live
e) changes in the parent/child relationship
f) taking risks
g) remaining active
h) making new friends – losing old ones and grieving losses
i) aging together by growing together as one adult to another

Communicating Clearly and Compassionately
Leaders teach and facilitate discussion and practice related to establishing the communication, acceptance, and work involved in developing a climate of acceptance. This climate is the context necessary to establish and maintain the relationships of fellow journeyers. The climate of acceptance embraces the qualities of patience, authenticity, respect, nurturing, valuing, gentleness, forgiveness, and loving humor. Such qualities are the ingredients of healthy growth and development – and of aging well.

Resolving Unfinished Business

Learning to relate to one another as adult-to-adult involves dealing with minor unfinished business as well as major life concerns we usually associate with death and dying. Participants are given individual and paired exercises to help them deal with questions related to unfinished business such as :

a) what do you wish you could tell the other?
b) what feels too 'petty' to bring up?
c) what do you need to explain?
d) what do you want to know?
e) what do you want the other to know?
f) where in your life do you need comfort?
g) what do you need to forgive/have forgiven?

Facing the End of the Journey

Participants are encouraged to explore their feelings about dealing with the inevitability that the 'end' of their journey into aging together will be death.

The leader(s) provide a safe environment and emotional support as needed during such exploration. Respect for individual spiritual beliefs is particularly important in dealing with this section. Death is not necessarily viewed by the participants as an 'end.' It is characterized for the purposes of this work as the end of the journey the participants mutually agreed to undertake as an adventure into aging together.

Participants explore such topics as:
a) opening your heart to one another and to life's beauty
b) talking to one another about your fears of dying and death
c) adapting to disabilities that constitute 'mini-

deaths'
d) making and discussing plans for funerals, memorials, and related topics
e) assisting one another in the grieving process
f) being actively involved in <u>living</u> until death

Like all effective interventions, "Aging as a Shared Journey" is designed to be a catalyst for changes people choose to make! We all age – we do have choices about how we age. Even when we face life situations that we must accept and cannot basically change, for example, some illnesses, we have choices about how we handle the circumstances.

Because there are so few examples to draw on, it is a pioneering act to explore the emotional territory that comes with being an adult child or elder parent. Spouses who choose to take this approach to their relationships may discover the joy of re-awakening some of the spirit of discovery that marked their earlier days together. Adult friends who agree to support each other's efforts to explore healthier options for aging well are likely to form new friends as well as strengthen the bonds of their long-shared friendships.

Taking a proactive approach to the quality of your life is a constructive stance. Sharing your strengths and supporting each other's changes enlarge not only your options but also your chances of success.

Readers are enjoined to be aware that the guide is a pattern that is whole and dynamic. Much of its strength lies in the way mastery of one portion reinforces success in another. It is imperative to respect the process and to understand that the use of the guide is an ongoing experience. Bear in mind that the parts are interwoven like threads in a tapestry. Persons who read the book as a self-help guide will ideally be doing so following workshop attendance. If self-help is your approach to the book, please be willing to seek guidance from a mental health professional if you recognize a need for increased depth or intensity.

Individual differences in ability to experience the book constructively will exist. Reader, I trust your good judgment to use this book wisely and well. The book, while it is very likely to lead you to a healthier, more fulfilling life, is not therapy, not counseling, and not a soporific.

It IS, however, an ADVENTURE! It is the beginning of AGING WELL, an approach that empowers you to be proactive in your journey into aging. It supports vital, conscious LIVING until we reach the end of the journey. Welcome, fellow journeyer!

Chapter 1: Heartwork

"...how tender can we bear to be?"
Rebecca Wells

This is the heart of the matter: aging is a journey we will make. If we are fortunate, and if we make wise choices, we will age well. Our choice is not whether to make the journey or not to make it. Our choice is how we will make it. The pith of the journey is in the heartwork – the love, understanding, acceptance, and compassion that we bring to the adventure.

Who will make the journey with you? Your parents, your spouse, your friends? You may have an elder or another adult who has already chosen to read the book and be your fellow traveler. If not, think as you begin your heartwork about special people in your life who are connected to you in the ways we discuss throughout the book.

Heartwork is rewarding, but it is not easy. With whom will you share your heart as you do your heartwork? You need not feel you have the answers to all these questions before you begin. Thinking so deeply about your relationships could

involve changing your perceptions of certain relationships. It will be helpful to keep an open mind
about who your fellow journeyers might be as you
read.

I recommend you do the exercises as you go
along. Giving yourself time to reflect is vital; this
is not meant to be read and shelved. It is meant to
guide you and your fellow travelers on your journey into the uncharted territory of aging.

Some of my clients, especially men, have told
me this 'heart-talk' is not the sort of thing that
grabs their attention. One university professor, Dr.
Ralph Tanner, prided himself on his intelligence
and logic – neither of which had provided the answers he was seeking about why he was so depressed. The day I met him, I asked him to describe
what he felt when he looked at his first wife's picture. "That sort of talk is just fluff," he replied.
"Don't insult my intelligence with that touchy-feely
approach!" I continued to talk with Dr. Tanner in a
formal, professional manner about my background
and credentials. As he relaxed, and we established
rapport, he asked me to call him Ralph and began
to show interest in working with me.

Ralph's first wife died of complications from
cardiac surgery eighteen months before I met him.
He had remarried within six months of her funeral.
As we continued our sessions, Ralph explored the
unresolved grief in his heart. He came to understand the pain he felt about his daughter's rejection of his second wife, Stephanie.

Just as Ralph did, the women and men who
choose to make this journey recognize that doing

their heartwork means emotional searching, decision-making, problem-solving, and risk-taking. It is far more complex than what Ralph once considered "fluff."

Recovering from a successful hip replacement, Ralph said he had expected to be home and dancing with Stephanie by a few weeks following the surgery. He was dismayed that he felt so tired that he had to be prodded by his Physical Therapist (PT). Ralph slept poorly; had lost his appetite; and could not "summon the will," as he put it, to work hard toward recovery. In addition, he was "insulted" that his orthopedic surgeon had allowed the PT to call me in for a psychiatric-mental health consultation. My being a faculty member seemed to make speaking with me at least more acceptable to Ralph, who had recently retired from a different college within the same university.

We began with a philosophical discussion about the heart as metaphor, in literature and in music. Ralph Tanner became an individual client, and he was intrigued that I was developing a guide for healthy aging. He wanted to work through some of his grieving for his first wife. He wanted to improve his relationship with Angela, his adult daughter, who intensely disapproved of his marriage to Stephanie. He wanted to enjoy a robust, healthy relationship with his wife of one year.

Like all of us, Ralph and his family had much heartwork they needed to do together. At the beginning, none of them would have characterized their being locked in to a 'tug of war' about how to deal with their grieving hearts as the need for heartwork. Ralph hid his hurt at the death of his first wife behind his proud "I am strong and healthy and much younger than my 70 years" stance. "Look at me," he said. "How can I be depressed? I'm married to a beautiful 45 year old woman! We give parties, play golf, dance, sail, and..."

Stephanie, hurt by Angela's rejection, was frenzied in her commitment to "keeping Ralph happy." And 38-year old Angela, longing for her mother's arms and needing to comfort and be comforted by her father, had frequent temper outbursts and raved about the insensitivity of her father and his 'new toy.'

Can you feel the pain beneath all those cries? Yes, their hearts were hurting, and their behaviors were efforts to stop the pain. You will have the opportunity to re-visit Ralph and his family in a later chapter.

Healthy aging is a way of life. It involves change and choice and courage – the courage to manage one's risks. The people you encounter in the book are protected by anonymity and minor changes in descriptions; but they are real people who experienced something of what you will experience as you read.

Think of your own life experience as you share what resonates with you about theirs – a circumstance, a feeling, a fear, a resentment, an unresolved issue, a longing for more! We will discuss various facets of the relationships described by the vignettes in different chapters.

Parents and their adult children have creative choices in how they experience the changes that accompany the parent's 'aging.' People in diverse relationships, for example, wives and husband, couples who are partners, and/or friends who are entwined in each other's lives, can choose to encounter aging together as pioneers helping chart the course.

When we become 70, 84, or 91, we begin to identify ourselves as people who are 'aging.' Despite knowing that we have, in reality, been aging since we were conceived, the term is typically used to describe old people. Why, when we are pre-teen and about to cross the threshold of puberty, do we not refer to ourselves as 'aging?' Why, when your parents are about to enter the arbitrary territory of "65 and over" do you refer to them as aging but fail to extend that same designation to yourselves, entering your 40's or 50's? Are not you also aging? Of course you are! So why is the term reserved only for elders?

For many elders, the true meaning of aging includes failing health, decline in the senses (especially of sight and hearing), limitations on mobility, and a host of losses, both major and minor. The losses, whether slight or great, have a cumulative impact on the quality of their lives, resulting in various kinds and disguises of depression. The recognition of what has been done and not done in their lives hits elders, sometimes like a sharp pain that almost takes their breath away.

Depression is a deterrent to positive response to medical treatment. My joint faculty appointment with the teaching hospital resulted in hundreds of referrals to evaluate depression in medical patients.

A few years ago, I was called to the hospital room of a 69-year old woman who was recovering from gall bladder surgery. Her nurse told me that the patient, whom I will call Vivian Powers, was recovering satisfactorily from her surgery. "But," the nurse added, "she has some things on her mind concerning her son that are agitating her. I thought it would be helpful if you came to see her."

The nurse decided to consult me because, as a geropsychiatric nurse specialist, I might be more acceptable to the patient who was accustomed to talking to the nurses. She explained to Mrs. Powers that I worked with older patients on psychological problems that were exacerbated by their hospitalization, as well as emotional issues that emerged in relation to coping with illnesses.

Entering the room, I saw Mrs. Powers sitting up in bed. She wore a pale-blue quilted bed jacket that complemented her overall well-groomed appearance. Her light brown hair was neatly curled under in a 1950's style pageboy, obviously held in place with hair spray. The television set was on, but she was not watching it. Instead, she stared vacantly into space. When Vivian Powers had her surgery, patients remained in the hospital longer than they do now, so there was more time available to address the emotional components of illness and death.

When I explained the purpose of my visit, Mrs. Powers' face flushed. She seemed embarrassed that she had revealed so much to her nurse. At first, she minimized her concerns. But in a little while, as we sat together, she released her pent-up feel-

ings. She was very angry with her son, Howard.
"When he comes to see me, he acts like he can't
wait to get out of the room. He wants to do what
he thinks is expected of him and get out of here as
fast as possible."

As she continued, Vivian grew more distressed
about her relationship with her only child. She
noted, painfully, that Howard had been trying to
get away from her for most of his adult life. Her
usual pattern of coping with his hasty getaways was
to distract herself from what she was feeling by
calling up her friends or by getting busy with something else. In the hospital, it was harder to do that.

The disruption of her usual activities, her concerns about surgery, and loneliness caused Vivian
to contemplate her health, aging, and the future.
The pain of her distanced relationship with Howard
swept over her. What had happened, she wondered, to that young boy she once thought she
knew so well? He was now a 45-year old man, and
she had no idea who he was. She worried that this
gulf would remain between them for the rest of her
life. She worried that she had accepted it so passively, not questioning why it existed.

When I recall that conversation with Vivian, I
think how emblematic it is for many parents and
adult children. An elder parent and an adult child
at mid-life have had a long relationship with each
other. Despite their familiarity, they may feel as
aging progresses that they hardly know each other.
I've heard adult children describe it like this – they
would be looking at a parent, and suddenly "see"
and old woman or old man. In a split second of
awareness, they wondered: Who is she? Who is he?

Parents can also be startled by such sudden moments of awareness, as Vivian demonstrated. One day, a parent looks at her adult child and the question occurs: Who is this grown man, who is this grown woman, who happens to be my child? Wives have told me of similar moments of sharp insights regarding their husbands. Who is this old man I've been married to for 58 years? Where did the boy I fell in love with go? Where did the child I poured my heart into go?

I think of these moments as the sudden recognition of "heart loss." As I have come to learn in my own life, if we don't pass over these moments too quickly out of embarrassment or discomfort, we will recognize a longing to know each other and to love each other as the adults we now are. And I think, with a quickening of my pulse, if we can dare to know 'the other,' we can dare to know ourselves as the adults we now are!

Often, we are not aware of the longing Vivian felt for her "little boy," Howard. Our attention is usually focused on mundane matters – living arrangements, health maintenance, and money. Sometimes we're embroiled in disputes that basically have to do with an imbalance between autonomy and dependence. Yet the anxiety we feel frequently stems from a wish to be known and appreciated by the other person, and a fear of separation that will ultimately come. Our wishes and fears can easily be absorbed, or cloaked, by practical problems.

Then, too, elders tend to think that by the time they have reached the seventh or eighth decade and their spouses or partners have also, or their children have reached middle-age, relationships are unlikely to change. If anything, elders and adult children alike fear that their present relationships will become more entrenched with age.

Sometimes this is true. But there is another way of looking at it. I like to think of relationships as a journey, because they are fluid. They are in motion, like life itself – marked by accelerations and slowdowns, tragedies and joys, and epiphanies and endings, with confusion at intervals along the way. As the noted psychologist Carl Rogers observed: "Life, at its best, is a flowing, changing process in which nothing is fixed."

While there is little doubt that older persons (as well as younger ones) can be very stubborn and rigid, knowing that the end of the journey is in sight can also be remarkably freeing. Certain things that seemed to matter so much before may not have much importance now.

Often we don't see ourselves in the larger picture until something happens to interrupt our daily routines. Most frequently, it is illness, or some other major event such as a significant birthday, or the loss of a loved one, which disturbs our usual way of coping. The parent cannot help but be aware that, under even the best of circumstances, the parent's days will end before the child's. The adult child cannot help but be aware that the parent will not always be there and that she will face her own death someday.

We are reminded of our own mortality in every relationship in which we are reminded of the mortality of the other. When we are parents, we approach such moments mindful that, like it or not, we still serve as models for our children. Vivian Powers' operation gave her the time to recognize that her relationship with Howard had become wedged in an unsatisfactory and even sad place. She decided to enter psychotherapy on a short-term basis to discover what was going on.

Initiating any change involves taking an emotional risk which is usually not an easy thing to do. Certainly it wasn't for Vivian and Howard. The difficulty lies in giving up what is known and venturing into the unknown. What if the new situation turns out to be worse than the old?

Another course of action may be to just leave things where they are. For some people, that may be a wise choice. But bear in mind, since we do not control what happens in life, not taking risks is a risk in itself. As psychiatrist David Viscott points out in his book, Risking, "If you do not risk, risk eventually comes to you. There is no way to avoid taking a risk."

I talked with Vivian about the approach I devised to help people learn to manage their risks, a method I named **RISC** and incorporated into the parts of my guide. We discussed the steps of the method, from which the acronym **RISC** was derived. Vivian was intrigued by an orderly way to approach her changes: 1) **Recognizing**, 2) **Inventory-ing**, 3) **Structuring**, and 4) **Choosing**.

Vivian had taken the first step: **Recognizing** she wanted more from her relationship with her son. She was willing to take the risk to make her

relationship with Howard closer and more meaningful. She asked me to work with Howard also, if
he was willing. I agreed.

When I first spoke with Howard, he was very
surprised that his mother was entering therapy.
Then he became concerned about what it meant in
terms of her mental health. Like many people,
Howard's preconceived notions about therapy
included a mistaken idea that only "crazy" people
seek therapy. Although the use of therapy to grow
and develop healthier lives is not new to Howard's
'boomer' generation, the information has not necessarily permeated that group sufficiently to be
integrated into their general knowledge about
mental health.

He wanted me to know that he was successful
in business and that he was capable of taking care
of his mother's needs. He would see to it, he said,
that she was provided with any "treatment" she
needed. The track Howard was on with his mother
was a conventional one. His relationship with her
was being organized more and more around
caregiving. As an only child, it was a point of pride
with Howard that he not neglect his mother. No
one could criticize him for not doing enough for
her. He was willing to give her anything she
needed, he said.

Howard was less willing, for some time, to
consider why he found it hard to be in the same
room with his mother, or even to acknowledge that
this was the case. As he and I talked, certain questions regarding his own feelings began to emerge:
why did he make the one-and-one-half hour trip
from New York City so frequently to see his

mother, only to rush away after a perfunctory visit? Why not visit less frequently if he was so busy in his business? Once having made the effort, why not stay long enough for a visit with more substance? What did he really want out of his visits?

By our third meeting, Howard was willing to talk more about himself instead of confining the conversation to his mother's needs. "I looked at my teenage daughters this weekend," he said, "and I realized I didn't want them to feel about me the way I feel about my mother. I am very uneasy when I'm with mother because I'm always waiting for her to criticize me. It's only a matter of time before she does. She's a very critical person. She divorced my father 20 years ago; but for 25 years before that, all she did was belittle him. I feel as though I've been wanting her to approve of me all my life. Now my daughters complain that I'm too strict with them and that I don't like anything they do." Howard conceded that he would have done nothing to initiate changes in how they related to one another, yet he was hopeful Vivian might change "before it's too late." Nevertheless, he was wary.

By even considering making a change in their relationship, Vivian and Howard were making a courageous move. Taking well-considered risks offers the prospect of a stronger and more enjoyable relationship which can help both parent and child deal with the challenges of life in a more effective fashion. However, I wouldn't deny that taking risks might produce new problems.

There are major risks for both you and your parents in letting each other know who you really are. The other person may find out more about

you than you are comfortable with, or you may learn more about the other person than you want to know. As a daughter told me recently, "I think I may not want to know who my dad really is."
There is a possibility of really disliking your parent or your child, or at least strongly disliking some of their values and behaviors.

Many times I have heard a mother say something to the effect, "I bite my tongue when I visit my son and his wife. I don't like what they are teaching my grandchildren. So I say nothing. But it's very strained." The parent in such a situation may fear that if she is more expressive and open about her feelings, she will reveal how critical she is. If you are the child of a parent who has been critical, perhaps you withhold information about yourself so as not to give your parent "bait." Certainly these were the dynamics of Vivian and Howard's relationship.

It may be helpful to know that taking a risk to alter a situation like the ones described in the book requires time. A risk doesn't take place in one moment. However, one change in a relationship frequently leads to more change. Indeed a kind of chain reaction of changes might be required before a relationship reaches a more mutually agreeable point.

If you are the person initiating change, one of the biggest risks you face is stopping at a point that is too shallow to really get satisfaction. The dynamics of changing the ways we relate to one another are so sensitive that I teach my clients the importance of taking such risks within the context of what I call "the climate of acceptance."

Creating a climate of acceptance facilitates the safety that is necessary for people in relationship to venture together into changes that can entail not only risks but also life-enriching possibilities. This climate is a compassionate emotional 'safe space' that both adults in the relationship agree to create as an expression of their loving concern for one another.

This climate is characterized by: nurturing, valuing, forgiving, sharing, caring, laughing, and renewing. The ways these qualities are fostered, along with suggestions on how to 'build' a climate of acceptance are integrated throughout the book. Vignettes, discussions, and dialogue from actual therapy sessions are given to help you understand how to apply the guide to your own life and/or the lives of your clients.

Vivian's determination to improve her relationship with her son gave her the courage to endure the pain of **R**ecognizing how she had treated him. "I knew from early on that my marriage was a mistake and that I didn't respect my husband," Vivian said. "I think I was afraid that Howard would turn out like my husband, so I put pressure on him to be better. In fact, I wanted Howard to be perfect. No matter how hard he tried – and I think he tried very hard – it wasn't good enough for me. All this time I thought I had put my ex-husband behind me, and here I was, letting my view of him determine how I treated our son," Vivian said with enormous regret.

Since Vivian's regrets made her tense, we decided to use a relaxation exercise to allow feelings of acceptance of herself and her son to surface.

Starting with her feet, Vivian first tensed then relaxed each muscle group in her body. This helped her to discern the difference between what it feels like to be tense and what it feels like to be relaxed. Through this exercise, Vivian recognized that when she was tense she tended to revisit past mistakes, which made her even more tense. However, when she was relaxed, she could be more accepting of where she was presently. Heartwork includes extending feelings of acceptance and tenderness to ourselves as well as to others who share our lives.

Once she was in a more relaxed state, I asked Vivian to write down an Inventory of her strengths. Her list looked something like this:

1. I have a son.
2. My son continues to try to relate to me.
3. My health is good overall.
4. I am young for my age.
5. I have several interests I can pursue.

Vivian felt better and better as her list grew. She was not only counting her blessings. She was creating a climate of acceptance of herself and others. She could see that she had a lot of pluses on her side that she could work with. She began to open her heart to herself as well as to Howard.

Later, using imagery as a tool, Vivian created mind's-eye pictures of how things could be between Howard and her. Talking about the way she formed thoughts of her son helped Vivian to cognitively restructure her view of him from "He's too much like his father," to "He's an individual man with his own set of needs and abilities."

Over time, the two essentially reintroduced themselves to each other. Instead of viewing Howard through the lens of her dissatisfactions, Vivian became curious about him. She asked him questions about his work and interests and listened attentively to his answers. Using the communication techniques and listening skills she and Howard were being taught, Vivian discovered a man she had never known. She was impressed with his accomplishments. By seeing him as a separate person and as an adult, Vivian found she didn't have to work to curb her tongue so much. She reminded herself from time to time that Howard was in charge of his own life and would make his own decisions.

Not surprisingly, Howard could spend more time with his mother without feeling extremely anxious. Eventually he was even able to cautiously inquire about her marriage to his father, and understand some of the difficulties of their situation. He was also able to appreciate the positive things his mother had given him and her concern for him despite her criticism.

Both became more accepting of what their stage of life demanded of them. The challenge to elders, as the psychoanalyst Erik H. Erikson wrote, is "to draw on a life cycle that is far more nearly completed than yet to be lived...to accept the inalterability of the past and the unpredictability of the future, to acknowledge past mistakes and omissions, and to balance consequent despair with the sense of overall integrity that is essential to carrying on."

By working on her 'task' of Integrity vs. Despair, Vivian let her age work in her favor. Accepting that she wouldn't be around forever, she knew she had only so much time to reconcile with her son. Instead of despairing, she allowed her age to give her the motivation to get going.

Howard was far more than a passive bystander. He allowed himself to open up, to feel his own hurt, and to see his mother as a person who had her own set of issues. His receptivity to change gave him a great deal of insight into how he interacted with his own children. Eventually, Howard and his mother were able to make the commitment to one another to travel together on their journeys into aging.

That commitment, when people in relationship make it, is a conscious pact with one another. It gets to the pith of the journey – the heartwork. It means that the people agree to make their journeys in loving relationship. Remember, our choice is not whether to make the journey or not to make it. Our choice is how we will make it.

When we choose to share our efforts to build and maintain a climate of acceptance and compassion, then by that choice we have made a commitment to travel together into aging. This choice means:

♦ We will be courageous. Certainly we will be afraid at times, but we will help each other cope with our fears.
♦ We will strive together to achieve what Carl Rogers called "unconditional positive regard." Our love for one another will be strengthened by each

of us granting the other the unconditional acceptance of being who we are.

♦ We will connect with and listen to our own hearts because this is the source of compassion. Listening to our hearts means being open to all aspects of our experience. This means not shutting out the parts of the journey we find painful.

♦ We will guide one another, lovingly. When we guide mistakenly, we will forgive one another.

Beginning Your Heartwork

I am not suggesting that you go at risk-taking relentlessly. My intention is to help you formulate ideas about what you want and to encourage you to set your own pace. If you think about how your relationship with your parent, child, spouse, or friend developed, it's clear that it did not happen in a moment.

Unless you lived in a very intense situation in which there was a concentration of pain and suffering, your relationship developed in waves – sometimes there was closeness and joy, at other intervals solitude or isolation, and at times discomfort and anger. Your current relationship may also have these waves. Changing its pattern will happen over time. But a commitment to change is necessary to realize beneficial results.

When people are doing the work of risking they sometimes find that it releases anxiety, or even panic, which can be a deterrent to continuing. Sometimes risk-taking taps into 'if only's,' as in "If only I had done such and such before." The longer one has lived of course, the more possibilities there have been for mistakes. It may help to know that the sadness over missed opportunities, as well as anxiety, may be only temporary. The fact that these feelings arise so readily may indicate that your old defense mechanisms aren't working so well anymore. This can be good. It indicates a strong desire to make changes and to develop healthier mechanisms.

If you have been in a very troubled relationship with your elder, spouse, or other adult, you may feel that Vivian and Howard's approach would not work for you. In fact, you may feel that it is necessary to 'divorce' your elder or other adults to get some peace. That is a risk you can take.

I talk more about forgiving the 'unforgivable' in Chapter 6, which deals with finishing unfinished business. Be aware that peace is not necessarily progress, nor does estrangement necessarily bring peace. A relationship can be very active emotionally even if the two persons never see each other.

Another course of action may be to just leave things where they are. Bear in mind Viscott's caveat that not taking risk is risk-taking in itself as you think about whether you wish to leave things as they are. Give yourself some time to let your emotions surface about how you really feel about staying in the relationship as it is now for more years to come.

Having talked about how one change begets another, I feel it is important to address the fantasy that any of us can change another person. While it is true that changes brought by one member of a family may provoke desired changes in another, you will not be successful if you set forth with a mission to change someone else. You cannot change your parent, your child, your spouse, or any other adult. There is only one person you get to change, and that is yourself.

If an adult wants to change, he or she has to be in charge of that change. If she or he does not want to change, then you might as well accept it and decide what work you want to do on yourself. In terms of parents, the older one is, usually the harder it is to change. If your parent has been behaving a certain way for 80 years, he or she may have little interest in changing and may lack the resilience to do so.

Having said that behavior entrenched for many years is difficult to alter, I still want to re-emphasize that, as Sarah L. Delany said at age 107, "we are never too old to change!"

If you are thinking that another adult is making you miserable, and you have tried to bring about change to no avail, you can at least change how you react to the other person. Whenever you change your behavior, you are changing your relationship. Your change, in fact, might inspire changes in the other person. But don't count on it. If it doesn't, your change at least means that you will be cutting down on your own aggravation by 50 percent.

For example, I know a mother who complains that her daughter nags her constantly. She feels she has tried to change communication patterns with her daughter along the lines that I suggest in Chapter 4. She says she has failed in her efforts to improve her daughter's communication. This mother may have to risk accepting that her daughter is going to be a nag. While she is trying to accept it, she may still get very upset with her daughter. She has some choices as to what she might do with her reaction.

First, I would recommend that she explore why she reacts as she does when she hears her daughter nagging her. She could think about what past events it recalls. Perhaps this woman felt the same way when her own father ordered her around. Any true insight into her reaction will be helpful. I say 'true' insight, because sometimes we are tempted to seize upon our most convenient rationalization and call it "insight."

The mind is too complex to lend itself to easy 'answers' and quickly-reached 'analyses.' Getting to know ourselves better involves paying attention to our inner 'voice' and balancing our self awareness with other information about our feelings, beliefs, and behavior. Much of that information is derived from feedback from others we trust who know us well, therapists and counselors, examination of the outcomes of our behavior patterns, and other sources we will examine throughout the book.

I would also recommend that this mother envision what she would like to do to her daughter when she nags. I think it is all right for her to acknowledge that she would like to slap her daughter, if that is true. Knowing she has the feeling is different from doing it. Certainly she should not use physical violence, but Recognizing her feelings may help her find constructive ways to deal with them. By being aware that she feels that angry, she then knows that she needs some way of managing her agitation. Perhaps she could find relief in furiously knitting, kneading bread aggressively, or other activities that can dissipate anger in constructive ways. Perhaps she needs to limit the amount of time she spends with her daughter.

Why shouldn't she take a creative risk to free herself from her usual response to behavior she feels is driving her crazy? She could ask herself, "What would I rather be doing than sitting here listening to my daughter nag?" Then she could go do it. It is possible, you know, to walk away from people when they are in mid-sentence. Obviously this is not the first choice of how to handle it. But sometimes things are so problematic that one has to temporarily go somewhere else, either internally or physically.

Making a change in your own reactions can feel like a risk. Of course the option exists to just ignore everything you don't like, or to complain a lot about the problems. Both these options also demand energy and they can consume the energy you might use to better advantage to initiate change.

Being a mature person you know that no relationship is just unmitigated joy. Anyone who describes a relationship that way isn't really in a relationship with another human being. Additionally, in these later years, there will be difficulties, if not some misery, to endure.

Even if you are fortunate and swim past illness and disability, there will be death to contend with. It looms so mightily that I suggest that both you and your elders address it as an issue in your relationships sooner rather than later. In the third chapter, I talk about how to do that. Given the vicissitudes of life, it helps wherever possible to contribute to the difficulty as little as necessary to accomplish your goals.

In terms of making changes, be attuned to your own pace. It is important that you develop trust in the process. I saw how different people approach change when I taught courses in assertiveness training. Some people found that if they acted brave, they then began to actually feel brave. Others needed time to feel brave internally before they could act brave.

There may be people reading this book who will have to think for a longtime before they feel ready to act. Have patience with yourself. Be patient with your fellow journeyers. Recognizing you have time to decide what approach may work best for you, take time right now to list at least two things you would like to be brave enough to change in your relationship with another, specific adult.

Changes in My Relationships "Wish List"

In my relationship with _____, I wish to change (describe)

In my relationship with _____, I wish to change (describe)

If you see yourself as partaking in a compassionate journey with your elders, spouse, or friends, you enhance your opportunity to grow spiritually. I am speaking here of spirituality in a broad sense, rather than referring to specific religious teachings. When I use the word spiritual in the book, it carries the meaning of one's sense of oneself in relation to one's world view; one's sense of purpose and the meaning of life. It is used in the context of soul-growth.

A compassionate journey has the effect of expanding the spirits of the people engaged in it. Think about ways in which you get in touch with your own spirituality. Prayer, meditation, music, concentration on nature, and many other avenues of access to our inner selves, our spiritual inner guides, are means in which you can get in touch with what is in your heart. List at least two activities that you use most frequently to become centered and in touch with your inner self.

I Become Centered, In-Touch within Me When:
- I pray
- I meditate
- I run
- I _____
- I _____

Think about the times you feel the most centered, peaceful, serene. What are you doing or not doing? How do you get in touch with your inner self?

Choose one of the methods you listed above, and enter into it now. Sit quietly. Breathe normally. Be still. Listen to your heart. What does it encourage you to do? What feelings emerge from feeling your oneness with your inner self?

Write something to yourself about what you are experiencing just now. Just write whatever comes to mind – it is up to you whether anyone else will see what you write. If the space below is too small, you may want to start a journal for the kind of responses you have as you go through this book.

In fact, I suggest you begin a journal and add to it as you read the book. It will serve as a tool you can use in many ways as you progress. Congratulate yourself that you are beginning your 'journey into shared aging' with enthusiasm! Your heartwork has begun!

Chapter 2: Relating Adult-to-Adult & Learning to Use RISC

*You are you and I am I
And if by chance we find each other, it's beautiful."
Frederick Perls*

This chapter is about the strengths of the adult-to-adult relationship. It shows that it is worth achieving even though it may be difficult to begin to alter the way each party sees the other. I will talk about how to recognize outworn behavior patterns that are limiting your relationships with your parent, adult child, spouse, or other important adult with whom you are in relationship. Once those patterns are recognized, I will show you some ways to implement and reinforce new ways of relating adult-to-adult. I will describe the *RISC* strategy that guides you and shows you how to actualize your new ways of relating.

Keep in mind the basic premise: aging and the changing balance of dependence/independence require new approaches to relating to others and to our communities. An adult remains an adult despite changes related to aging. Aging well requires learning new ways of relating that are congruent with maintaining our identities as adults. The choice is to make the journey as collaborators, with adults committed to changing, learning, risking, and problem-solving within the context of a climate of acceptance.

Within our families, all adults – children and parents, husbands and wives – are aging. Nonetheless, at any age, a parent is still a parent; a spouse is still a spouse; a friend is still a friend; a lover is still a lover. Participants are encouraged and guided to undertake the journey in the spirit of shared adventure into aging which they choose to make together. I stress the importance of remembering as they go along that each person has made a choice to work together.

Choice is an important ingredient of the climate of acceptance. This is especially true when the fellow journeyers are parents and their adult children. It might seem that being at different stages of life would inevitably create a gulf between them. Of course, sometimes it does. But in my experience working with adult children and parents, both are buoyed tremendously in their respective challenges if they can release outmoded roles and establish a sense of connection.

The simplistic notion that a 'generation gap' creates a chasm that cannot be bridged is more often a defense against doing the heartwork of relating – the hard work of opening up our hearts to feel what lies within them and to share what we find about our true selves. Today's elders constitute the most differentiated, or heterogenous, group of people in any age cohort.

The differences in the way elders have related to the historical period in which they have lived and in the growth and development they have experienced are far more likely to impact their world view and values than their chronological age. As you continue with your heartwork, try to avoid stereotyping your elder fellow journeyers and insist that they avoid stereotyping you or your generation.

Creating a climate of acceptance involves a mutual commitment to learn how to nurture, respect, accept, and support one another. As you examine your attitudes, values, and expectations with a willingness to view one another as adults, both you and your elders will gain a lot of freedom of action. There are numerous ways to increase understanding and acceptance, such as writing letters to one another; role-playing different styles of communicating; role-reversal exercises; and sharing stories and mutual interests like movies, sports, crafts, or books.

If you find that there is a great deal about your parent or any other adult with whom you are in a significant relationship that really irks you, such as the other's lifestyle or choice of friends, it's time to sit down and try to recognize what is going on. If you feel that another adult's behavior is 'driving you wild,' 'wearing you out,' or somehow blocking your ability to live your life, then it is a good idea to spend some time looking at the dynamics of your relationship. The two of you may be struggling over who is the adult and who is the child – who is going to be the 'parent.' Yes, the two of you may be locked into a power struggle that you had not recognized for what it is until you began to think about relationship issues such as the ones we discuss in the book.

In terms of power, the parent-child relationship is by definition unequal. It is a hierarchy with the parent having a certain amount of control over the child and the relationship. Parents set standards for their children and may make certain demands of their children. This is not unlike the stereotypical marriages of the early 1900's in which the husband had a certain amount of control over both his wife and his children and over their relationships. The father set standards for the wife and children, made certain demands of them, and 'ruled' their lives from his strong patriarchal stance, however benign his benevolent 'dictatorship' may have been.

Parents also try to protect their children from physical harm and from emotional trauma. A parent may rush in to rescue a child from emotional challenges that seem too difficult for her. Parents make decisions about what their children can handle. While this behavior may be appropriate when the child is young, it is a set-up for a power struggle between a 50-year old child and a 75-year old parent.

The adult-to-adult model is much more egalitarian. The adult-to-adult approach, or model, assumes that each person has more or less successfully completed earlier developmental stages. It assumes that each person has an identity – she knows who she is. In the context of a climate of acceptance, differences in the needs, limitations, and resources available to the adults involved are viewed as bridges – not barriers.

For example, a mother who can no longer drive may be perceived by her adult daughter as 'another obligation.' The mother may perceive herself as becoming a burden. However, if the two have agreed to create a climate of acceptance, they can view the times the daughter drives the mother as opportunities to explore topics that can strengthen their emotional ties. They will also have the freedom to explore new and different ways for the mother to travel, thus reducing her dependency on her daughter to provide transportation.

In our society, we can get quite muddled about dependence/independence issues when a parent needs help or care-taking. Mainstream American mythology holds that every adult is self reliant, so we equate dependency with childishness. We forget and sometimes disguise how interdependent most of us are physically, financially, and emotionally. Just because we depend a great deal on each other does not mean that we are not responsible for ourselves.

Even if your parent depends on you for certain things, you need not feel that your parent is becoming a child. Rather, she or he is an adult who needs assistance. Part of your job is to find ways to provide assistance without losing sight of the maturity of the parent(s) you are assisting. Your parent also has a job – that of working out how to appropriately receive your assistance.

My graduate students helped me heighten my awareness of how what I call 'mainstream' culture in this society differs from many smaller groups within the United States. For example, an Asian student wrote an erudite paper on the problems faced by Asian parents transported here by children who become U.S. citizens. When the high value given to the parents' honored place in the family is threatened with the American "I'll do it my way" attitudes adopted by their children, parents cannot understand their relationships with their children. Both generations suffer the consequences.

There are many such examples, and adults who choose to work with this guide should begin by making a list of comparisons between the cultural values about old people that belong to their home of origin and those that exist in their adopted home.

Because there is so much confusion about the meaning of independence, dependence, and interdependence elders have good reason to fear that their autonomy will be snatched away from them if they are physically dependent. The fear that their children will become their 'parents' and begin making all their decisions for them is well founded in reality. Stubbornness may be the only way an elder knows to fight back.

One the other hand, I have known elders who think they are still the boss of their adult children. They are still expecting their children to 'obey' them and be everything the parent wants them to be. I've heard elders say to adult children, "I don't know where you got that. I didn't teach you to be that way." I say to parents, "you must understand that by the time a person is 50 years old, you can be certain he has not been influenced exclusively by you."

When both parties are adults they have more freedom to be who they are without worrying about loss of self. They can be spontaneous and humorous. They can share their anxieties with each other. They can give each other help in working out problems, but they can also give each other space to work out problems for themselves. When you are dealing with an adult, you don't necessarily have to rush in to rescue the other person. You can convey that you have confidence in the other person's ability to tolerate frustration and to handle certain difficulties.

There are risks in letting your parent, your adult child, your spouse, and/or your friends know who you really are. Participants in this journey into healthy aging are guided in doing an assessment of their readiness to take such risks. Those who begin by attending an "Aging as a Shared Journey" workshop are given a specific form to help them assess their readiness.

Reading this book and/or working with a counselor or therapist are other ways adults are guided to think whether they are willing to begin planning risks they will take to change their lives. If they agree they are ready, they are taught how to use **RISC** by applying the four steps that are described in depth in the last section of this chapter.

Risking Changes in the Parent – Adult Child Relationship

In an adult-to-adult relationship you and your parent change the way you relate to one another, yet she continues to be your parent. Your parent needs to increasingly view you, the child, as also an adult. The parental stance must soften and recede into the background. As the relationship becomes more grounded in an adult context, parents have less need to 'declare' from a parental posture and become increasingly willing to treat you with adult respect.

By the same token, although the child may see a parent losing certain strengths and abilities, you are mindful that you are still dealing with another adult. Your parent is always your parent. Fear of losing that connection is often at the basis of the elders' reluctance to learn new ways of communicating with their children and is sometimes a fear shared by their children.

A major task of the transition to adulthood is taking the responsibility to 'own' one's life and to be accountable for one's choices. As an elder, you must realize that your child has a right to be different from you. Parents I work with can typically accept this more easily if they think about it as extending to their adult children the same kind of courtesies they extend to their friends. We don't get and keep friends by being judgmental or telling them how they must live. We get friends by being more accepting.

Acceptance and approval are not synonymous terms. A parent may or may not approve of her child's life choices. People vary in their values, and the values parents choose for living their lives may or may not be the same as their child's values. This is difficult for parents, especially those who cling to beliefs in how their values have shaped their children in order to bolster their own self-esteem. When such conflicts occur, working through them within a climate of acceptance can strengthen the bonds between parents and children and launch them on their shared journey into aging.

In many families, essentially the same values are shared and passed along for generations. There are examples of families in which several generations develop in that way, without compromising the authenticity of any of the family members. Conflicts usually arise, however, when an adult child makes life choices that are incongruent with parental values. When that happens, both parents and children can choose to continue to love and accept one another.

Both generations can find ways to respect the other's right to embrace its own values. Some of the case vignettes in later chapters will give you examples of how differences in values between parents and their children may be resolved. You will meet Annabel and Mack, a mother and son, and Lionel and Lionel, Jr., a father and son, whose stories illustrate the role of compassion and acceptance in resolving differences.

It can be remarkably difficult to see the need for change in ourselves. Here is an incident from my own life that relates to how difficult it can be. We were fighting again, my daughter and I. Angry and confused, I thought: "She's a woman in her 40's now. I believed that we had weathered the worst and had come to a place in our lives when we could enjoy an adult-to-adult relationship. What's wrong?"

That encounter took place a few years ago. When I hung up the phone, my stomach was churning. It was an ironic position for me to be in. Much of my most rewarding work has come from helping older clients to negotiate more equal relationships with their adult children. But when it came to listening to my own daughter, I stopped thinking and started analyzing. "She's tense," I conveniently told myself. "Her attack on me indicates stress-related regression to earlier, more adolescent behavior."

That's when the alarm sounded! Wait! Wasn't I analyzing her in order to avoid feeling hurt by what she said to me? That was what she had told me – almost word for word. We had both been angry on the phone. I had told her that she was resentful because I disagreed with her. "All right," she retorted, "analyze me and get it over with!"

She, too, was seeing that our conversation was following a typical pattern. Much of the time we got along fine with each other. Trouble arose whenever we differed significantly on an issue. We would argue, and then she would tell me that I was acting like a know-it-all parent. I would get mad at her for hurting my feelings and then feel guilty about what I had said to her. Shifting back and forth, I would first vow to get even with her for complaining about my behavior; and then I would worry about how to make up.

I had thought that my relationships with both my daughters were adult in every respect. Certainly we had all worked diligently and consciously toward that goal. That's why I was surprised by a flash of insight showing me that a part of my relationship with my elder daughter was stuck in an adult-younger child mode – a not uncommon situation for many elders. Finally, I laughed as I recognized that I was the one behaving like an adolescent.

Laughing at myself assured me I would survive the moment – and that my relationship with my daughter would improve. The ability to laugh at oneself while also respecting oneself is a component of healthy aging.

You may find that there are things about your behavior or even your character that your parent does not like at all. Well, where is it written that the people we love will always please us? Love paves the way for tolerance and also for appreciating the good in one another. But you can't know what you will appreciate about your parent or what she may appreciate about the person you are unless you take an interest in each other's lives.

There are plenty of elders who just stop listening when an adult child tries to share his or her work life or social life. These parents act as though they expect all their conversations with their children to center on the mother's or dad's life. By maintaining this position, your parents are missing out on knowing who you are. Some of the communication exercises I teach my clients help parents and children learn to be accepting about each other's lives.

I am not suggesting that relating adult-to-adult means that parents and children should become 'pals.' Your life experiences are such that it is inappropriate for you to be 'just pals' to one another. Your relationship is enriched by the parent/child bonds that were formed earlier and can continue into adulthood, though perhaps expressed differently. Your parent will be your parent even when you have become a parent as well.

For elders whose children have children, it is wise to keep in mind that grandparents who relate in healthy ways to their own children are far more likely to nurture healthy relationships with their grandchildren. Stereotypes like the 'doting grandma who spoils' or the 'indulgent grandpa who gives the child everything he wants' are not helping build healthy families. Instead, they are helping build emotional cripples.

Adult children must be willing to change some of their beliefs about their parents as well. Emily and her mother, Ruth, each had work to do on themselves as I taught them how to use this guide to improve the dependence/independence balance in their relationship. Their story illustrates some things adult children must realize. For example, you may be a person with years of experience living as an adult and still find yourself hiding facets of yourself so as not to provoke your parent's anger or disappointment.

Emily, a married woman in her 40's whose only child had just gone out on his own, spent much of her time at her mother's house. She insisted that her mother was too frail to manage alone because of her heart condition. However, Emily resented the time and effort she spent shopping for Ruth, cleaning house for her, and protecting her from overexertion.

Emily had long planned to fulfill her lifetime ambition to become a writer once her son was 'launched,' and while her husband was busily engrossed in his successful career as a middle manager in a large company. Just as she reached that point in her life, her mother was hospitalized with an irregular heartbeat.

Ruth was discharged the following day, and she told Emily she had been warned to 'protect her weak heart.' Emily, who had not shared her dreams of becoming a writer with her mother, resigned herself to her understanding of the "caretaker role." Silently, she decided "to put my life on hold once again," she told me.

"I worry constantly about mother falling on the steps or collapsing trying to get to her bedroom on the second floor," Emily said. We explored the information about Ruth's condition, and I learned Emily had not spoken with the physician herself. She had not asked for a diagnosis or pressed her mother to explain why she had not been placed on any medication. Emily's fears were based on Ruth's statement about protecting her weak heart. I asked Emily to help me understand why she seemed so compliant and anxious to do everything for her mother without questioning her involvement.

Emily's brief reply spoke volumes: "I do what I can to avoid mother's criticism. She's always been on me about being a good daughter, and I am an only child – like my son." We discussed that it is difficult if a parent has maintained a habit of being critical of you, of admonishing you for things you have done, or of trying to get you to follow orders. To alter the relationship meant that Emily would have to assert herself more as an adult. "Perhaps you can reassure your mother that living your own life does not mean you will desert her," I suggested.

Emily was surprised how easily her mother agreed to come in with her and talk about whether they wanted to contract to work with me to learn to continue their journeys as partners in aging. It is not unusual for both parties in a relationship to be ready to change but unable to open up to one another about doing so. When they understand that using the shared journey guide can give them something akin to a map to follow, they are likely to feel empowered to try.

Once both Emily and Ruth began expressing their concerns, I introduced them to the *RISC* strategy. They were able to see that, by **R**ecognizing things that worried them, they had already begun the first step in that process. By working through their relationship, Emily and Ruth found that they had more choices than they realized about how to structure their lives and how to relate to each other.

Previously, both were too busy focusing on their preconceived notions to really analyze Ruth's physical health. Once liberated from that struggle, they began to visualize and deal with how to improve Ruth's environment. The detailed medical information they got as part of taking their Inventory helped them release unnecessary anxieties about Ruth's heart condition. Emily was able to share her dreams of becoming a writer with Ruth, who found those dreams exciting.

Now they have help for chores. By moving Ruth's bedroom to the ground floor, Emily no longer feels she has to be constantly available to help her mother. As a result, Ruth feels more independent and able to take care of most of her own needs. Moving toward a more equal way of relating that was no longer exclusively a caregiving arrangement, both women became freer to enjoy each other's company as adults. Each of them discovered through improved communication that the other was more interesting than either of them had realized!

Emily learned, as many children do, that even if you are critical of your parent, or your parent is critical of you, or even if there are things you definitely do not like about one another, making an attempt to be more open gives your parent a chance to be more open with you. As a more adult, objective listener, you may discover things to admire or appreciate about your parent.

And as you continue to work on being nonjudgmental of one another, your parent is likely to find things to admire or appreciate about you. By not showing yourself, you make it impossible for your parent to appreciate you as an adult. By taking the risk of showing more of yourself, you are likely to gain more of yourself.

Risking Changes in Other Adult Relationships

When we are truly engaged in life, the **RISC** process cycles over and over. Its desired outcome is to have more choice in life and in how we age, and to feel less at the mercy of often bewildering feelings and events. For that reason, examples of **Recognizing, Inventorying, Structuring,** and **Choos-**

ing are threaded in and out of the whole fabric of the pattern for the journey.

It is typical to harbor preconceived notions about 'what if' we were to change? Looking at those preconceived ideas helps us begin to Recognize our fears and take a good look at where our resistance to change lies. Stop now and think about some preconceived notions, or beliefs, you have about the important relationships in your life. Use the form below to capture some of your thoughts for later reference in your journey.

PRECONCEIVED NOTIONS

Write your statements below:

I believe that if I were to

the result would be (describe below)

1.

2.

SAVE THIS FOR FUTURE REFERENCE

When two adults who live together and/or spend most of their time together see each other as adults, both gain from their relationship. The story of Mabel and Ed illustrates a married couple who regained their adult perspective of one another. Sitting at a table in a senior center, I asked Mabel, a 76-year old woman, to tell me about her husband, Ed, who was playing dominoes at a nearby table. "Well," Mabel said, "you know Ed's 88 now, and he's just a broken down old thing. He can't remember where he puts anything, and he forgets to go to the bathroom soon enough so he dribbles on his clothes – things like that."

"What was Ed like as a young man, say, when you and he got married?" Laughing gently, Mabel replied, "Lordy, that was almost sixty years ago, Hon." A silence ensued as I sat, aware that Mabel had been transported back in time by the power of reminiscence. Her eyes held a little twinkle, her slight smile was pronounced; her face was serene.

After a few moments of reverie, Mabel said, "What a handsome fellow he was! All the girls wanted to catch him. He was fun, and smart, and ambitious – and strong! Won the weight-lifting contests at the County Fair nearly every year. And, oh, honey, he was so loving..." Mabel's voice trailed off and her face became sad as she clearly recognized the contrast between young Ed and the 88-year old man sitting stooped and looking lifeless at a table near ours. "Thinking about changes you see in your husband seems to bring up some sadness for you," I said quietly – and waited. With a sigh, Mabel replied with a tone that held tears in her voice, "Yes, I call him my baby now."

Mabel's life had changed from the vital woman with a vital husband to a tired, dejected old woman with a 'baby' to care for in her old age. Mabel, at that time, had no idea how much she and Ed were short-changing themselves by playing out their stereotypical roles for their life scripts. In fact, she had no idea she was scripting her life. The passive role of the 'woman's place' that had seemed to work for Mabel when she was married to a strong man who could 'lead' her into an active life had gradually metamorphosed into a drab existence in which she wiped his chin and reminded him to go to the bathroom.

Ed and Mabel were both victims of their own ageism. The of Mabel and Ed is an example of how people can change their lives by changing the way they relate to one another. It also illustrates how viewing the strengths in a situation can result in an increase in wellness for elders.

At times, a parent becomes autocratic and stubborn with a child, or a spouse with a spouse, because that is the person's way of maintaining control of his or her own life. In the case of Mabel and Ed, I learned that when Ed began to decline physically, he initially tried to 'order Mabel around.' Although Mabel had accepted – and even welcomed – her husband's leadership throughout most of their marriage, she had not perceived Ed's way of being the husband as 'dominance' until his frailty became so much more evident.

The adult-to-adult approach allows each person to be in charge of himself to the degree possible. It allows both adults involved to behave more like partners or allies rather than rivals for control. More decisions are made by negotiation than by fiat.

When Mabel decided she wanted to find out if Ed could be helped to become more like 'his old self,' I asked a colleague of mine, a Physical Therapist (PT), to do an assessment of his physical functioning. My cognitive examination of Ed showed that, while his memory had deteriorated, some return of more effective memory function was possible if Ed were highly motivated. The family physician confirmed our findings that no evidence of neurological or other disease had been detected, except for chronic arthritis that had been diagnosed when Ed was 73 and hypertension that was well controlled by medication.

The PT put Ed on a rigorous program of bladder re-training and overall strength enhancement. Ed was motivated by his love for Mabel, who became his 'coach,' encouraging him with kisses, praise, and occasional sweets for dessert. Mabel was motivated by the satisfaction she received from seeing her husband become less a victim of learned helplessness and by the goals she set for herself as she learned she had choices about what she would accept about the meaning of being old.

She learned how ageism is a prejudice shared not only by the youth but often by the very people who are elderly. She learned how the beliefs we hold about our life scripts (the stories we believe about how our lives must work out) can be modified to take more advantage of our strengths. Mabel proved to be very adept at setting goals for making small, but meaningful, changes in her life script. One of her favorite sayings, remembered from somewhere though the author was forgotten, was "I want to wear out – not rust out."

Ed and Mabel were not an exceptional couple. They were, as Mabel said, "just regular folks." The changes they made in their relationship resulted in improved quality of life for them and increased confidence in 'aging as a shared journey' for me. The changes took place over a period of about a year, and improvements came in small increments.

There is no 'quick fix' and no magic to this approach. Nonetheless, the last time I saw Mabel and Ed they were on their way to a neighborhood square dance, and their relationship was restored to an adult-to-adult balance. Yes, she still re-minded Ed to wipe his chin occasionally – she finally remembered, she always had! Finally, she could remember it with her healthy sense of humor restored. Humor is another vital ingredient in a climate of acceptance.

Learning to Use the RISC Strategy to Improve Adult-to-Adult Relationships

RISC consists of four steps: 1) **Recognizing** 2) **Inventorying** 3) **Structuring** and 4) **Choosing**. Recognizing how we feel about the changes in our lives is not as simple as it may sound. For example, awareness of failing health may seep into our con-sciousness gradually, as was the case with 38-year old Margaret, who was diagnosed with multiple sclerosis. She said, "I was working too hard, and I knew I needed to change something, because I'm not 19 anymore. Every time I had a weak spell, and that time I slipped going upstairs, I pushed back my fear and promised myself I would slow down."

When Margaret fell down and was unable to get back up, her husband found her on the floor and rushed her to the hospital. After she had time to digest what her physician told her about her diagnosis, Margaret was able to recognize that she had 'known' something was very wrong for some time.

Emotional problems are often even more difficult for people to recognize than physical problems. Symptoms that signal depression, for example, or other conditions that need attention, such as severe anxiety disorders, are likely to be perceived as discomfort that must be endured. You would be wise to familiarize yourself with some of the material distributed by organizations like the Mental Health Association about recognizing mental illness. Fear of mental illness is a major cause of failure to seek treatment early enough to take preventive measures before psychological symptoms become severe enough to warrant a diagnosis of mental illness. The value of paying attention to your mental health and proactively maintaining it cannot be overemphasized.

⇒ Recognizing

In the beginning, I teach my clients how to recognize the traps in which they are caught. An emotional trap may be a fixed idea – something like "I am too old to buy new clothes." The trap may be a situation, such as family dynamics that involve subtle patterns of abuse. False beliefs or misinformation like believing there are no resources when, in fact, possibilities do exist, can also be traps.

Once traps are recognized, I encourage my clients to make a list of everything they can **R**ecognize about their current situation — feelings, thoughts, beliefs, fears, facts, or anything that is meaningful to them.

As time unfolds and people continue to work through the steps, they learn that **R**ecognizing and the other steps need to be repeated in a somewhat cyclical manner. Living is dynamic, not static. Old habits change, new behaviors are learned, and outmoded coping strategies give way to healthier ones as elders and the adults close to them embrace opportunities to live more vital, healthier lives.

⇒ Inventorying

EMPHASIZING A FOCUS ON WELLNESS AND HEALTH IS NOT A TECHNIQUE FOR GLOSSING OVER REAL PROBLEMS, BUT RATHER A WAY OF PUTTING THE WHOLE PERSON INTO PERSPECTIVE.

It is important to make a realistic Inventory of one's personal aging, an assessment which does not cover up the problems and fears of aging with a bright veneer of platitudes.

Sylvia, whose leg was amputated due to complications resulting from diabetes told me, "Well, now I'm a cripple." It was true that now she had only one leg. It was a fact that she faced arduous physical rehabilitation and the need to learn to walk with her prosthesis. Inventorying (Step 2) begins with making an inventory of strengths. Guiding her through this step, I coached her to Inventory her strengths. Her Inventory led to a more holistic description that went something like this:

1. I am a wife.
2. I am a mother.
3. I am a friend.
4. I am a violinist.
5. I am an avid reader.
6. I am a woman who has only one leg and needs to learn to cope with this.

It is equally important to Inventory problems that need solutions, but one of the best things we can do when we want to make a change is to start with our strengths. Yet few of us actually do this when we try to tackle a problem. There is a tendency to zero in on how bad things are and become demoralized and frozen. This is why the inventory embedded in the *RISC* process is so important. It paves the way for motion rather than stasis by helping people in distress assess what is good about their lives.

When doing your Inventory, you should include a health inventory that lists both your health problems, if any, and your preventive health habits, like good nutrition and exercise, that are among your strengths. In order to further maximize your forward motion, your bridge to the next step will be to prioritize how you plan to use your strengths. For example, Sylvia decided to return to her beloved violin playing to reinforce her awareness that she was still the accomplished musician she had been most of her life.

⇒ Structuring

During this step, the Structure of the relationship is actually changed. Like every step in the process, it occurs over and over in the dynamic and

ongoing growth, learning, and 'journeying' together. As the adults who are shaping the adventure relate to each other on an increasingly accepting, nonjudgmental, and egalitarian basis, the
relationship takes on more dimensions and involves more options for how it can be Structured.

One of the most helpful aspects of including
Structuring as a specific step is that by doing so,
you reinforce your confidence that you will always
have choices. Achieving mastery by using the strategies and making commitments to continued use of
the guide will reinforce your strengths, yet Structuring the relationship remains a life-long challenge.

I encourage people to think about building the
Structure of their relationship as being somewhat
analogous to building with 'toy' construction
blocks. When the 'blocks' no longer serve the function you wish, or when you think of more creative
ways to arrange them, structure them differently.
Doing so is often a difficult challenge, and the
process can become so uncomfortable people will
cease for a time. Be alert to distinguishing between
taking a break and going into a downward spiral
when discomfort arises.

No matter how hard the Structuring becomes, I
encourage people to keep in mind that by exerting
some control, some choice, about how they respond
to their lives, they are maintaining autonomy and
independence in the healthiest sense of those
qualities. I also encourage people to use health-
producing humor in their Structuring plans. Many
of my clients are adult children and their parents
who learned how to laugh and play together when

mom was '75' and daughter was '56'!

By what you Recognized in Step 1, you will have become aware of some problems in your relationship with your parent, spouse, or other adult that you want to improve. By doing your Inventory (Step 2), you will have become aware of strengths you have to address your problems as well as barriers that you must overcome in order to make your desired changes. Step 3 begins as soon as you and your fellow journeyers are able to formulate a plan for how you will build on your strengths to change your relationship in the manner you have chosen. At the end of your Inventorying, you will have prioritized how you plan to use your strengths. Your choice of top priority will often become the focus for the beginning of Structuring.

With respect for differences and the variables in relationships, all people who are learning to use *RISC* are guided when Structuring their relationships to do at least the following:

a) Plan how you will build on your strengths
b) Agree on how you want your relationship to function
c) Decide what your 'building materials' will be – journals, study, workshops, counseling, prayer, body work, therapy, retreats, other
d) Spend scheduled time on strategies to improve communication, as well as using those strategies in your everyday interactions with one another
e) Plan periods of rest from the work to have fun together
f) Be authentic, clear, and compassionate with one another

g) Remain mindful of the importance of doing everything in a climate of acceptance
h) Recognize when one or both of you need help – there is no 'macho' prize for doing this work (is there a female counterpart for 'macho'?)

⇒ Choosing

You have already made a number of choices by the time you begin working on this fourth step. It is included in the strategy to guide you in focusing on the specific choices you make about how you will continue to structure your relationship and accomplish your goals with your fellow journeyer. You have agreed to work mutually to learn and apply the **RISC** strategy as you work through the sections that make up the pattern of the journey.

The choice to be fellow journeyers in "Aging as a Shared Journey" implies other choices. They are:
a) To be partners throughout your mutual journey of aging
b) To be pioneers in relating to one another adult - adult while respecting your roles as parent - child, spouse - spouse, or friend - friend
c) To remain committed throughout life to a compassionate journey
d) To explore and to change as you grow and to give one another the freedom to grow
e) To support, nurture, and forgive one another

Mabel and Ed chose the strength of their marriage over many years as their top priority when they listed their Inventory of strengths. During Step 3, Structuring, I guided them in reminiscence and arranging a collage of pictures that depicted some of their best 'marriage moments.' That activity was done cautiously, with awareness that comparing the past times with their present state could exacerbate Ed's depression or trigger increased sadness for Mabel. With the focus they had chosen, they were able to agree on specific goals for rejuvenating their relationship.

Moving into Step 4, **Choosing,** they planned activities to enrich their time together, capturing the essence of their former, healthier marriage. A major choice involved Ed's agreement to work diligently with his Physical Therapist. Related to the physical strengthening and training, the couple made a choice that Mabel would be Ed's 'coach.'

Adult journeyers who make the five commitments listed above must recognize the importance of remaining true to their mutual contract with one another. Some of my clients have made observations like, "My goodness – I didn't think about my marriage vows as hard as I'm thinking about doing this!" This step involves being very specific about implementing the choices you have made. For example, a son and his father listed as one of their goals for **S**tructuring their relationship, "Spend more time doing things together that are fun." That deceptively simple goal involves, at the very least, the following decisions:

a) how much time is "more time?"
b) what activities do you consider fun?
c) are you willing to choose spending time with the other trying something he considers fun but you do not?
d) how many weeks you will try out your plan for fun activities before you evaluate the

impact it is having on your relating to one another?

When a list such as the one above is read from a dispassionate, objective perspective, it appears so evident you may question the need for being so specific. It may be helpful to keep in mind that when you and your parent or other adult are actually doing this work, you are doing so within the context of an emotionally charged relationship. Attention to specifics helps you communicate clearly, increases the chances you will succeed, and helps you become more sensitive to the difference between relating as you did in the past and consciously Choosing how you will relate to one another.

From your experience, it will be apparent to you that the Choices with which you will more likely be dealing in your life are far more complex and sensitive than the above example. Some of the Choices that relating adult-to-adult most frequently involve are those that are inherent in changes, negotiations, decisions, and agreements about:

a) living arrangements
b) management of finances
c) handling of illnesses and/or disabilities
d) resolving long-standing family conflicts
e) management of children and grandchildren
f) becoming more interdependent
g) handling arguments and disagreements
h) understanding each other's values and spiritual beliefs
i) advanced directives and funeral plans
j) disposition of family heirlooms and things of sentimental value
k) resolving unfinished business about secrets

l) concern about how health issues interfere
with aspects of their relationship they value

m) disagreements about habits, for example.,
smoking

n) changing habitual communication patterns
that are outmoded

o) grieving and losses

p) dying and death, or 'facing the end of the
journey'

Take a moment to stop here and think about
what you would add to the list above.

Get quiet; breathe normally; think peacefully as
you continue.

Now compile your own list, then prioritize the
list by assigning #1 to the most important, #2 to
the next most important, and so on.

Relating adult-to-adult is a continual challenge
to keep your hearts open to one another, to be
forgiving, and to deal with one another compassionately. Remember to check out the state of your
climate of acceptance regularly, to be authentic, to
respect differences, and to keep your strengths in
mind. Be open to learning new communication
skills, doing the exercises suggested in the book,
and looking for lifetime learning classes that can
enhance your journey.

Have fun together! Keep in mind that you have
made a commitment to go into this pioneering
venture as a SHARED journey – you will find the
terrain hard at times, but you are not alone! Be
aware you may need a counselor, a therapist, or
spiritual guide to help you – if so, be certain to

choose one who shares the values inherent in "Aging as a Shared Journey." If you have not already begun keeping your journal, now is a good time to begin!

As you continue to read and explore each section of the guide, the glimpses into people's lives provided by the case vignettes will illustrate the reality of aging as a shared journey. The elements are the framework that guides the journey. *RISC* and other strategies, exercises, and activities are the tools used to assist in the journey. The more you give yourself to the process, the more creative you become in devising your own tools and strategies. The possibilities are endless – not daunting, but encouraging prospects that add 'spice' to the journey you plan to make!

This is a good time for you to stop reading and practice going through a simple experience with *RISC*. Remember the value of small steps. If what you tackle at first is too large, you will be more likely to think the process doesn't work for you. Trust me – it works for everyone. Tailoring it to the individual and the needs of a particular situation is where the behavioral science comes in. Still, aging is both an art and a science, and you can begin with it from 'where you are.'

1. RECOGNIZING - be specific. Write ONE sentence that describes something in your life that you wish was better. Make it realistic, not: "I wish is was a millionaire". Make it something like "I wish my mother and I could have more fun together." Your sentence describes as aspect of your life that you Recognize could be more fulfilling.

2. INVENTORYING - be specific.

a. List the strengths you can contribute to what you have wished, for example, fun. This is the beginning of your Inventory.

b. List the strengths your other (for example your mother) can contribute.

c. List the resources you and she have, such as "we can both get to the library to look up activities that could be fun."

d. List the potential barriers to your wish (for example "she thinks things are funny that I do not").

3. STRUCTURING - be specific.
Write your answers to these questions and add any other ideas you have:

a. What is one specific activity you wish for?

b. What specific activity does your other wish for?

c. Beside each potential barrier you listed in the Inventory, what changes could you make to overcome them? Here is an example:
Barrier: Time
I would need help with the children
She could give up some TV watching
We could communicate more openly about how we each spend our time
We could agree on a mutual time to start and finish, and how often we would meet.

4. CHOOSING - be specific.
Write your choices in affirmative sentences, each beginning with "I choose _____" Here is an example:
I choose to spend one evening every two weeks with Marie. I choose to stick to our

agenda for having fun, and not to use that time to discuss family problems, worries, or to 'grind' any of my 'axes', like "I wish she would let her hair be natural and stop coloring it that awful color."

Chapter 3: Meeting the Challenges of Aging & Illness

*"Everyone who is born holds dual citizenship,
in the kingdom of the well and in the kingdom of the sick."*
Susan Sontag

This chapter will explore points of view of illness and disability from the perspective of elders and of the adult children, spouses, and others who are in relationship with them. There are very real aspects of physical aging that challenge the relationships between you and your elders. Even aspects of aging for which it is possible to compensate, for example, glasses for changes in vision, serve as reminders that make denial of aging more difficult. Illness and disability test relationships. In this chapter, we will examine the adult-to-adult approach as it relates to caregiver relationships, and we will look further into using **RISC** to help us cope with illnesses and disability.

The degree to which inevitable changes impair our health is related to our proactive health practices, e.g., avoiding obesity, not smoking, and to our emotional outlook on life. A mentally healthy adaptation to the changes that we must accept as we age takes advantage of certain attitudes. One of these is optimism. It is usually found in the company of a healthy sense of humor, another contributor to aging well. Laughter, as Norman Cousins demonstrated years ago, is healing. The action of laughing improves our circulation and breathing and reduces stress.

Bandura and other researchers have shown that a person's belief that he or she is capable of a change in behavior (self-efficacy) is correlated with whether that individual will make the effort to change. Seligman and others have studied correlations between emotional and physical well-being and such psychological states as helplessness. It is now generally accepted that positive attitudes like optimism, hope, and confidence have a favorable influence on longevity, health, recovery from illness, and adaptation to disability. Optimism and pessimism were once believed to be immutable positions people take toward life, but they are now recognized as choices amenable to change. This knowledge has enormous implications for enhancing our health and wellness.

Think about how you see elders treated in our hospitals, senior centers, nursing homes, clinics, and even in families. What evidence do you find that they are encouraged to feel capable, exert their autonomy, believe in themselves, look forward to their future, and enjoy generous doses of healthy laughter? How could you be a positive influence in these areas?

An elder's awareness of failing health often triggers anxiety, dread, and other emotions as well as 'takes the lid off' repressed childhood fears of vulnerability and helplessness. The facts received from physicians and other health care providers are often heard through a screen of anxiety. "The growth is cancer," is likely to be quickly translated to "I am going to die." The meaning we attribute to illness and disability is related to how we have coped throughout our lives. Our characteristic ways of responding to stress influence our perceptions of what it will mean to become more dependent, face limitations, or change our lifestyle. An elder's preconceived notions about how loved ones will react to her/his changed health conditions sometimes result in disaster predictions. Disaster predictions sometimes result in self-fulfilling prophecies. The ramifications can go on and on.

When illness or disability are becoming a major challenge, there is no substitute for a thorough and accurate geriatric assessment of all systems, including neurological and psychological. In some parts of the country, special clinics are available for comprehensive geriatric assessment. The Claude Pepper Foundation is a well known source of excellent geriatric clinics, research-based programs, and other activities germane to enlightened geriatric treatment. You should be able to obtain information about Pepper centers and/or other geriatric medical facilities in your area by contacting a university program on aging, a graduate program in gerontology, or your nearest Area Agency on Aging.

Where geriatric clinics are not available, you may need to assist your elder parent or other adult and their health care providers by insisting the primary physician refer them to appropriate specialists, e.g., psychiatric professionals. Psychiatry and geriatrics are medical specialties. Not all physicians are well educated in those fields, anymore than all physicians are well educated in obstetrics or orthopedics. Dangerous myths abound, both among the professional community and in the general public regarding symptoms that are attributable to aging. Aging is a normal process – not a disease!

Aging and Ageism

The term 'ageism' was coined in 1969 by Dr. Robert Butler to denote prejudice and bigotry toward elderly persons, akin to racism and sexism. It refers to discrimination against people on the basis of their age. Erdman B. Palmore, a gerontologist who has studied ageism extensively, defined the term as " any prejudice or discrimination against or in favor of any age group." The negative ramifications of ageism support and perpetuate the myths that endanger the health of elders.

Some of the most frequently encountered myths are listed below. If a physician, nurse, or other health care provider tells you they are facts, change providers as quickly as possible. Ignorance, no matter who harbors it, is hazardous to our health! Any knowledgeable Geriatric Psychiatrist, Geriatrician, Geriatric Nurse Practitioner, Clinical Nurse Specialist in Psychogeriatrics, or Family Practice Physician will confirm my statements about these myths. If you wonder whether information you have been given is accurate, you should always insist on a second opinion. This list is not exhaustive, but it will give you some idea of the kinds of misinformation you may hear.

a) "Depression just goes with getting old."
b) "Confusion is normal when people get old."
c) "Memory loss is just to be expected."
d) "When old people's taste buds begin to atrophy, they just lose their appetite."
e) "Not sleeping well is just a part of being old and having lots to worry about."
f) "Loss of interest in sex is to be expected."
g) "A lot of people who had pleasant personalities when they were younger get irritable and agitated when they get old."
h) "The medicines we have to give them do keep them very drowsy."
i) "We use restraints on their arms and legs because it's safer for them."

You have a right to question any statement that includes "...it just goes with aging" and to ask for references where you can learn more about the changes. Physiological, psychological, social and environmental changes take place throughout our entire lives. Although such changes can have a cumulative effect over time, you should remain cautious about what you attribute to the fact of chronological aging vs. what deserves more thorough evaluation, assessment, and recommendation. For example, depression is so well recognized as an illness that exacerbates many medical problems that it is discussed in a separate section later in this chapter.

In helping elders in your life adapt to illness and/or disability, the more you know about who they are, the easier it will be to choose actions that constitute actual assistance rather than an invasion of their rights as adults. Learn what their values are, discover what they consider 'quality of life,' and try to understand their world view. There are great differences among elders. One 83-year old man may feel his ability to read, spend time with his dog, and watch sports on television provide him with a satisfactory or even very good quality of life. On the other hand, his 83-year old neighbor may consider life hardly worth living if he can no longer ski, fly his plane, and drink a six-pack of beer every weekend.

Stereotypes about the elderly negate the vital facts of how different people actually are. For instance, quality of life is a subjective term, and you cannot correctly make assumptions that an elder's limitations make his/her quality of life untenable. What appears untenable to you may feel acceptable to the elder. The elder's perception of quality of life will have a strong influence on her/her ability to adapt to diminished health or to limitations.

Another important consideration is that adaptation takes place over time. For example, when Sylvia initially learned she had to have a leg amputated, she said life without both legs would not be worth living. As she began to work through *RISC* with me and to respond to physical therapy and rehabilitation, she discovered that being able to continue to play her violin, spend time with her grandchildren, and volunteer at the library provided her with a very satisfactory quality of life.

Communicating compassionately, making shared decisions, and working out solutions together are helpful and effective ways you and your elders can choose to respond to the changes necessitated by illness and disability.

The Adult-to-Adult Focus and the Caregiver Relationship

In the case of parents and children, deteriorating health and impending disability threaten to convert the relationship into a reverse child-parent paradigm centered on caregiving. How the parent and child respond to illness can help strengthen the relationship emotionally or can plunge it into a pattern of avoidance.

You may have heard something like this yourself, perhaps in a supermarket, a park, or in a physician's office. An adult child admonishing an elderly parent, saying in a strident voice something like, "Mother, I <u>told</u> you to use your walker!" The tone of exasperation has a familiar ring, similar to the tone you might have used with a three-year-old: "I <u>told</u> you never to cross the street by yourself!" Comments such as this, delivered by a caregiver, mean she is probably embroiled in an autonomy-dependency struggle with the elder. This kind of struggle often emerges when an elder experiences illness or disability or becomes frail. Some physicians, nurses, or other well-meaning health care providers actually encourage such power struggles without recognizing what they are doing. "Well, he's just getting old now; you will have to take over," my father's physician once said to me when he was sweeping my father's arthritis under the rug of 'getting old.'

A child, spouse, or other caregiver who mistakenly follows such advice will soon find her toler-

ance ebbing when the elder fails to respond 'favorably.' An ill or disabled elder needs time to adapt
to health changes while continuing to function as
much as possible as the adult he has been for many
years. With the adult-to-adult approach, he will be
given time to adapt and opportunity to participate
in the decisions being made about how his illness
or disability will be handled. Adults who assume
the caregiver role often find their initial good in-
tentions, tolerance, and benevolent feelings turning
into resentment, impatience, and frustration more
easily than they could have imagined.

In most cases, adults do not enjoy being
infantalized. This term means treating adults as if
they have become infants when they need help
with bathing, toileting, walking, or other activities
of daily living. This behavior damages an adult's
self esteem and contributes to regression or rebellion, and sometimes to cycles of both reactions. It
is important to watch for infantalizing behaviors
and correct them as soon as possible. Some examples are: using 'baby talk,' patting their buttocks
when changing undergarments, shaming, and
calling them 'pet' names. An elder may need extra
help or extensive care, but he or she is still an adult
with experience of adult autonomy. It is healthy
for an adult to resist being reduced to a dependent
child

Consider what a person is going through who
is vision impaired and cannot drive, who can no
longer walk safely without a walker, or who can no
longer hear what people say in everyday conversation. A loss of physical functioning feels like the
beginning of a downhill spiral. To an elder, the loss
of a function can feel like a mini death. This loss

can be so traumatic that the elder resists by refusing to acknowledge loss of function, refuses to use a walker or a hearing aid, or 'forgets' to take medication. It is not unusual for daughters and sons to perceive such behavior as their parent's 'rebellion' against them. Consider the parallel between viewing behavior as a power struggle intended to 'rebel' and the interpretations parents often place upon the behavior of their adolescent children. In my experience, elders are more often 'rebelling' against the downhill spiral of aging they fear, or resisting giving in to a mini death – perhaps taking the poet's advice, "Do not go gently into that good night!"

If you have a parent who is ill or disabled, then you have the problem also. Much has been written about caregivers and caregiver burden. You have probably heard the term 'sandwich generation' to refer to adults who are 'sandwiched' in between the needs of their aging parents and those of their children. Some of the books that are most congruent with a mentally healthy approach to being a caregiver for your parents are listed in the references for this chapter. Of course, I omitted those that emphasize 'becoming your parent's parent,' because I strongly disagree with that way of thinking about becoming a caregiver for your parent.

Today we hear a great deal about persons who are hired to assist elders tread the murky waters of declining health. In an increasingly mobile society, there are often geographic barriers between children and their parents who need help. Even when children live near their aging parents, the demands of their careers, child raising, community involvement, and other activities often necessitate their hiring someone to assist the parent. As Health

Maintenance Organizations proliferate, the services of some sort of 'manager of health' may even be required in order to obtain necessary health care. We use terms like 'case manager' and 'care manager.' At the risk of having my mail box filled with irate letters, I maintain the position that the children and other loved ones of elders who need help should avail themselves of such services from a 'buyer beware' perspective.

The very term 'manager' calls into question precisely what and who is being 'managed.' I maintain that an elder is an adult who has managed her or his own life for 60, 70, 80 or more years. The need for assistance in continuing to do so does not obliterate the need to consider the elder's personality, quality of life preferences, and the myriad of other things that make up the elder's life.

Usually, an elder's family or close friends have years of valuable experience getting to know these things about the elder's history. Your familiarity with your elder's story is a mine of knowledge for persons caring for your elder.

Contribute information about your elder's preferences, strengths, past achievements, interests, and ways of coping to case managers and other health care persons involved in your elder's care. You can help them discover creative solutions to some of the dilemmas they experience when working with your elder. For example, an elder with advanced dementia may have a stuffed animal that has been treasured for years. Placing a comforting 'Linus blanket' in her/his arms when you see the first signs of agitation may help. Transferring affection to stuffed animals that symbolize our sentiments about people and/or times in our lives is quite common. We do not lose the consolation we derive from having our favorites to hold when we become adults; we simply stop talking about it so we won't be considered childish.

Show pictures of your elder as a healthy, vital adult to the health caregivers. Share with those who help care for your elder brief anecdotes that assist in perceiving your elder as an adult. Be brief, keep in mind that caregivers have many tasks to perform and many people for whom they provide care. Remember that people, circumstances, adaptation to illness and disability, and resources available in a given setting are widely different. Showing respect toward your elder's caregivers will help them respect your elder as well as your special place in your elder's quality of life.

Applying the RISC Strategy to Adapting to Illness and Disability

When you have come to a point in using **RISC** that the choices you make have become actualized, it becomes clear that you have reached the end of one **RISC** process and the beginning of the next. Life is not neat, so typically, you begin another cycle in the midst of completing the one you are working through. Do not try to order your life to fit the steps in **RISC**, as doing so would be futile in any case. You need to become so well acquainted with this approach that whenever a Recognition strikes you, it becomes an automatic signal to get in touch with your feelings, beliefs, and values about what you have **Recognized**.

Next, get started on your **Inventory** related to what you have recently recognized. Your Inventorying will point the way to what needs to be **Structured** differently in your life. Your **Structuring** will lead you to the Choices needed to achieve the new Structure. And so forth. Remember that your Inventory includes what resources you need to help you work it through – a therapist, a medical examination, a friend, a minister, a reference book, or all of the above.

Elders and their children, spouses, or other caregivers can use *RISC* to help them adapt to changes in a healthy manner. When Emily and Ruth, whom you met in Chapter 2, first learned to use *RISC*, they **Recognized** that they had been so busy resisting each other's choices about how Emily would care for Ruth that they had not even checked carefully to learn exactly what Ruth's condition meant medically, or to what degree she actually needed help with her activities of daily living. This is not uncommon. People sometimes ask me, "Well, isn't it obvious someone would have to start by **Recognizing** what situation they are in?" Apparently not. In my experience, the stress of acknowledging illness and potential decline is so great that anxiety quickly 'takes over.' Sometimes, facing illness and its implications vacillates with denial, and we need to be patient as elders adapt to what is happening to them.

In addition to the emotional effects, there are other factors involved in the need to take a careful approach to *RISC*-ing. For example, Vivian, whom

you met in Chapter 1, needed to focus on her unresolved feelings about her husband in order to work
out her relationship with her son, Howard.

Recognizing how we feel about the changes in
our lives is not as simple as it may sound. It is
often necessary to identify which feelings are responses to health changes and which are symptoms
of depression. Treating the depression may be the
first priority so that there is energy and focus to
work with *RISC*. The word 'depression' is used
across a wide continuum of feeling, ranging from a
clinical diagnosis of mental illness to a transient
period of disappointment. Using the one word
indiscriminately for the broad range of depressive
symptoms compounds ignorance with confusion.
Therefore, it is wise to seek the assistance of a
mental health professional to help evaluate symptoms and discuss whether treatment for depression
is indicated.

Today's 70, 80, and 90 year olds are likely to
believe they must simply 'put up with' depression.
Even worse, their families and health care providers
often share that misconception. Depression is not
a normal correlate of aging. The losses people
experience as they become old certainly result in
the need to grieve, but the normal grief process
should be acknowledged and approached differently than a depressive illness. This is important
even though the two conditions can, and often do,
exist simultaneously. We will talk more about
depression later in this chapter. We will talk more
about grieving in the last two chapters.

Inventorying always includes listing the
strengths the elder brings to the situation. For

example, elders who have kept to a fairly regular exercise routine prior to the onset of illness probably have the strength of better muscle tone and overall fitness to help them adapt to the accompanying changes. Elders who are accustomed to approaching challenges positively and who believe that it is possible to compensate for limitations imposed by illness or disability should list positive attitude and belief in overcoming limitations as strengths. Elders whose lives have included a grounding in spirituality bring the strengths of faith and spiritual practice to their ability to cope with illness or disability.

The Inventorying involves listing facts about the illness and/or disability. Health care providers and family members need to help elders with this part of the Inventory. The information must be accurate, the options outlined in clear terminology, and conflicting information examined carefully. Care must be taken not to provide too much information at one time because that can be overwhelming to the elder, especially if the elder is frail. Frail elders are often mistaken for being unable to participate in their decisions when the real problem is 'drowning' them with information overwhelming to the elder.

Remember to think broadly and include the elder's friends, interests, personal characteristics, and health care resources. Social support systems are vital resources that may be unavailable in the traditional 'neighborhood' sense. Instead you might need to look for help for social support from churches, students studying aging, telephone contacts, computer linkages, mail carriers, senior centers, school children, and so on.

Structuring includes helping people make specific plans for use of the strengths and resources that have been inventoried. In this step, we help the elder Structure his/her transition from the 'old self' to the *self-in-becoming*. Transitions and change are inherent in living, but the anxiety and uncertainty that can accompany changes are often particularly frightening to older people. It is important to explore ways to 'let go' of old behavior and manage the anxiety of what William Bridges has called "the confusing nowhere of in-betweeness." Once we let go of old patterns of responding and managing our lives, the energy that is released permits us to go forward toward our new goals. This means creating new patterns of behavior, or new Structures.

There are many possibilities for getting in touch with the *self-in-becoming*. I use guided imagery to help people get in touch with the self they would like to become. Guided imagery is facilitating the use of the 'mind's eye' by inducing relaxation and providing a graphic description of an image that forms in the relaxed person's mind's eye. The particular images used are related to the personal characteristics and goals of the people involved.

It is important to be realistic. No amount of guided imagery will turn a 5 feet, 4 inches woman who weighs 160 pounds into a trim one who is 5 feet, 11 inches tall and weighs 110 pounds. No form of mind's eye exercise will turn a 74 year old man into a 24 year old 'jock.' What is more, in working with hundreds of elders, I have learned that such drastic changes and idealized goals are not important. Most people do not expect 'magic,' and people will usually be pleased to see incremental changes they can accomplish toward their goals.

You can apply these ideas about using *RISC* with elders in transition when you are making changes or experiencing transitions in your own life. I assure you that self-doubt is normal at this transitional time in the *RISC* process. It's as if the concept of self that has been the underpinning of self-esteem for years crumbles before there is a clear picture of the *self-in-becoming.* To bridge this transition, I teach how to evoke what Dr. Herbert Benson calls the relaxation response.

Once that is mastered, I offer a smorgasbord of techniques for stress reduction to help my clients through this process. In the next chapter, you will read more about learning to relax, using various stress reduction techniques, and using guided imagery to develop a mind's eye image of your *self-in-becoming.* The ability to communicate clearly and compassionately begins with becoming centered and quiet within oneself. Your *self-in-becoming* arises from the quiet place within you that is your inner presence, a place you access by first becoming relaxed and letting go of tension.

Choosing, the fourth step in *RISC,* encompasses a plethora of options, which can be overwhelming, but it need not be approached with alarm. The whole of this step, and the choices within it, is made up of many smaller steps. I encourage people to visualize stairs of different sizes and heights. Stepping off a platform that is 12 feet from the floor may result in breaking bones. On the other hand, stepping from one step to another, one step at a time, on a standard stairway is not likely to result in injury. Like Bill Murray in the movie, "What About Bob?" you may want to take 'baby steps.' If you are coaching your elder loved one to take small steps, be careful how you use the phrase 'baby steps.' You should avoid terminology that suggests infantalizing the ill or disabled one.

Making choices about health habits and ways to respond to health challenges is akin to being able to choose what we want in life. Although it is not synonymous with having everything we want, it is powerful enough to draw fulfillment and joy into our lives. I emphasize the value of elders making decisions about the quality of their lives. I believe they need to define choice in relation to the realities of their health, resources, and emotional needs. They need to be willing to examine their closest relationships to determine whether those relationships are supportive of their making healthy choices. Couples, for example, who have lived for years empowering each other's illnesses, may resist making healthy changes in their lives. On the other hand, think about how Mabel and Ed Chose to cease focusing their relationship on Ed's failing health and began making healthy choices that enriched their lives.

By Choosing preventive health practices we have some influence on which health problems we may face during our lives. An obvious example is making a choice to stop smoking. Becoming aware that we can Choose how we will respond to whatever health challenges come into our lives or those of our loved ones has a positive impact on our mental health. A mentally healthy approach to living involves viewing ourselves as whole persons

– body, mind, and spirit. Such a perspective on who we are is referred to as a holistic health perspective.

When someone tells me something like "I am a cancer patient," I ask them questions like "How is your spirit responding to the cancer?" and "What do you think about when you think about being diagnosed with cancer?" I want to encourage them to perceive themselves as being more than a disease, as being whole people who happen to have a disease. From a holistic perspective, we are able to identify with the health that is in us, or 'own' our health, despite illness and/or disability.

Depression

As a psychotherapist, my entry into people's lives is often at the point where they feel overwhelmed and depressed. Treating the depression may be our first priority. Depression is not a normal result of aging. Elders who come to the attention of the medical professions have, on average, two or three medical diagnoses. Depression is frequently either a contributing factor to their medical conditions, a closely associated reason their medical conditions become worse, and/or a condition that complicates their response to medical or surgical treatment. Despite these facts, depression's contribution to medical illness is often either ignored or minimized.

Symptoms of depression are a factor in illness that simply must be recognized, and treated. In an effort to refute my consultation recommendations, a prominent physician once said to me "...why do you go on about her depression? She's 81 years old and sick! OF COURSE, she's depressed!" I've heard many versions of his response. My answer to him bears repeating here: "Her being 81 years old does not present a reason why she must suffer from symptoms of depression that could be relieved. Her medical illnesses do not have to be exacerbated by her depression. If her depression were treated, she could have more reserves with which to cope with her other illnesses. Why must she suffer more because we won't treat her depression?"

There are different beliefs among health professionals about the best approach to treating depression. I try to avoid getting stuck in black/white categories, i.e., treating with pharmacology vs. treating with psychotherapy. I recommend a holistic treatment approach that may include medication, psychotherapy, spiritual counseling, stress management, support groups, and complementary treatments, e.g., therapeutic touch. There are often compelling reasons to relieve symptoms as rapidly as possible so that the depressed person's resources can be mobilized toward health.

Brief psychotherapy is useful for either elders who are taking medications or for those who do not require medication. In my experience, I find brief psychotherapy in conjunction with supportive immersion in teaching and using *RISC* is particularly effective with elders. Depending on the severity of the depression, the education may either follow positive response to psychotherapy or be used simultaneously. A sense of 'running out of time' is often expressed by my elder clients. Their concern about 'getting on with' improving the life they have left appears to influence their amenability to a blend of supportive and cognitive brief psychotherapy.

In situations where a clinical depression has become so deep that the client's cognitive processes are significantly impaired, there may be immediate need for medication. When symptoms are so severe they must be ameliorated before my client and I can use *RISC*, I collaborate with nurse practitioners or physicians who can prescribe appropriate medication. Once the elder begins to grasp the principles of this kind of work and has enough energy to start using them, we begin working through *RISC*. Mabel, whom you met in the second chapter, said, "Well, if you can do what you do pretty fast, I'll try it. After all, I'm 76 years old now – if things are going to get better, let's hurry; Ed and I may not have much longer."

It is not unusual to find that the hardest part of treating elders for depression is convincing them it is possible. Soon after they begin the work, this method of coaching them along tends to bring them relief that reinforces and encourages their continuing. Begin with a keen awareness that it is important to recognize and respond quickly to depression. Seek the assistance of your health care provider and/or a mental health professional that you trust to obtain information about treatment options appropriate to the form of depression you or the elder you are helping is experiencing. Be alert to the presence of four or more of the following symptoms:

DEPRESSION*

The experiences below are not listed in order of importance. Just note whether you have experienced them for a period of at least two weeks within the past four months, or whether you experienced two-week periods on a recurring basis over the past year. Check each one that applies to you or your loved one. If you check four or more, talk about it with your primary health care provider for further consideration of the possibility that options for treatment of depression need to be considered.

1. ___ depressed or irritable mood (or both) most of the day, almost every day
2. ___ fatigue or loss of energy
3. ___ loss of appetite, especially for food typically enjoyed
4. ___ marked changes in ability to enjoy or be interested in acitivities usually pleasurable
5. ___ significant weight loss or weight gain not associated with dieting
6. ___ difficulty sleeping nearly every night, or alternating sleep/wake short periods
7. ___ feelings of worthlessness, helplessness, or helplessness almost every day
8. ___ difficulty thinking or concentrating, or indecisiveness, nearly every day
9. ___ preoccupation with thoughts of death or morbid thoughts about life almost daily
10. ___ thoughts about suicide, recurring notions related to ways to kill oneself
11. ___ withdrawal from talking with people normally contacted by telephone or visits
12. ___ sustained loss of humor in situations usually considered amusing or funny
13. ___ neglect of personal hygiene, e.g. bathing,

changing of underwear, washing hair, etc.
14. ___ lack of interest in appearance, e.g. make-
up if usually worn, matching clothing, etc.
15. ___ prolonged inattention when someone
you love is relating something to you
16. ___ morbid or frightening dreams, e.g.
dreaming you are drowning
17. ___ neglect of a pet typically in your care, e.g.
forgetting to feed your dog
18. ___ thinking one or two thoughts over and
over, like they are "stuck" in your brain
19. ___ physical agitation, e.g. frequent pacing,
jerking movements, startling easily
20. ___ dreading to get out of bed in the morn-
ing and face another day

* This questionnaire is to be used for screening
your experiences and it is NOT diagnostic.

Common Responses to Illness and Disability

Knowing what changes normally occur as we
age can help you identify those that are attributable to a specific illness or disability. Your response will be conditioned by whether you perceive
what is happening as a normal part of the aging
process or as an 'insult' inflicted by illness or disability. The following table shows the most common changes that take place during the process of
aging.

NORMAL CHANGES OCCURRING WITH AGE

PHYSIOLOGICAL CHANGES
Sensory Changes
Vision
More light is required to see. Color fades or disappears. Changes in the lens of the eyes lead to decreased peripheral vision, light accommodation, and reading ability.

Hearing
Nerve changes may result in reduced perception of high-frequency tones and consonants (e.g. "red', 'bed' and 'dead' may all sound alike). Background noise will more significantly interfere with reception of foreground speech. These changes require more energy for attention and unscrambling of what is heard, and may contribute to confusion, "inappropriate answers" and/or rigidity in thought processes.

Taste
Decreased acuity as taste buds become less sensitive. Person may be less aware of seasoning in foods and the nuances of enjoyable taste differences.

Touch
Increased sensitivity to light touch and to pain on touch. May become less aware that arms and legs hit objects, e.g. hitting a door when walking through it.

Smell
Diminished sense of smell. May result in safety hazards, e.g. failure to smell smoke,

failure to recognize spoiled food, etc.

Cardiovascular Changes
Heart
Output of energy and blood flow through the heart may decrease as the heart loses some of its elasticity. The heart may become less responsive to increased demands. The heart valve changes may result in benign heart murmurs. <u>There are not changes in resting heart rate associated with aging itself.</u>

Blood Pressure
Changes occur in blood vessels resulting in increased blood pressure, which can lead to an increased pulse rate or slightly irregular pulse.

Blood vessels
Arteries may become blocked due to increased thickness of the walls and/or to build-up of fatty deposits on the interior wall surface.

Respiratory Changes
Chest muscles
Chest wall may become more rigid, resulting in more pressure against the lungs when expanded. The pharynx and larynx muscles become weaker, increasing difficulty with swallowing. Respiratory accessory muscles may become weaker.

Lungs
Blood flow within and to/from the lungs becomes slower. Lung tissue becomes less elastic, reducing effectiveness of breathing.

Skin Changes
The texture of the skin becomes less elastic, leading to wrinkles and lines. The color changes resulting in paler face and spotty skin pigmentation. Fat distribution changes to less on the arms and legs and more on the trunk. Nails and hair growth rate decreases and hair color and distribution change. Skin temperature changes result in cooler extremities and decreased perspiration.

EMOTIONAL AND SPIRITUAL CHANGES

Family Relationships
Studies have shown that recently widowed white males are at greater risk for suicide than the risk in the general population of elders. Both women and men who maintain close ties with their children and grandchildren remain healthier emotionally and spiritually than those who are alone and lack friends or other support systems.

Lifelong Adaptation
Elders who have been active and curious, seeking learning opportunities, and being involved in their communities and religious activities during their lives tend to remain active, providing the challenges of illness and disability are managed. There is some truth in the axiom many of us have heard, "people die like they live."

Preparation for Dying/Death
Elders who have a terminal illness and/or condition that causes them to experience dying and death as a reality soon to be experienced may seek spiritual meaning and deeper emotional involve-

ment than they have ever experienced and actually become healthier in that realm than they have ever been. Dying can be a growth experience.

Meaning-making

As Carlsen's research has shown, elders who are successful in finding meaning in their lives tend to be emotionally and spiritually healthy. Elders who fail to experience life as meaningful comprise the roughly 10 15% of the elder population that experience some form of depression that is not linked to physical changes in the brain. These estimates vary with research methods.

Many elders were taught to 'pull yourself up by your own bootstraps' and to equate asking for help with weakness. Often older people are not comfortable asking for help or sharing their emotional vulnerabilities. Sometimes shame about needing help can lead an elder to ignore important needs and seek attention in other, inappropriate ways. That can lead them to withholding information about their situation, or refusing to use medications or devices that can help their functioning.

By not being candid because they "don't want to be a burden," elders may unwittingly deprive their children, spouses, or other significant adults of an opportunity to help them in ways that could help you both be more at ease in the relationship. In other words, your elder's inappropriate effort to 'go it alone' will be a barrier to your building healthier adult-to-adult relationships.

The opposite side of the coin of exaggerated independence is what Seligman termed "learned helplessness." Walter, for example, had been steadily acquiring a learned helplessness in relation to his wife ever since the onset of his Parkinson's disease. Walter's wife, Eloise, had always had a tendency to be controlling. When he became ill, the couple fell into a more pronounced dominant/subordinate pattern. Walter gradually became aware that he wanted a more equitable relationship even though he was dependent on his wife for specific kinds of help.

Once Walter recognized his healthy desire for more autonomy, we inventoried his strengths. Inventorying his strengths led to a realistic way to communicate to Eloise what Walter could actually accomplish on his own, or with minimal help. Before he shared his inventory with Eloise, Walter expressed anxiety about how she might respond to it. He related numerous arguments they had about what he could or could not do on his own, or with minimal assistance.

Walter and I did a reverse role-play in which I 'played' Walter and he responded as he believed Eloise would respond. We worked on Walter's communication about his desire for increased autonomy. We worked on how he would share his strengths Inventory with his wife. We talked about the importance of the exchange taking place in a climate of acceptance. When we had the necessary ingredients for acceptance and openness in place, Walter and Eloise participated in the role-play with me as coach. The relief that spread over Eloise's face when she fully realized her husband wanted to relieve her of the burden of helplessness was beautiful! You will read more about this couple in the next section, "Climate of Acceptance."

Elders may feel very absorbed in their illness or loss. Low self esteem contributes to the feeling that they are isolated in their pain, sadness, or despair. Particularly if an elder has lost a spouse and friends to death, she or he may believe that no one in the younger generation can identify with how desperate they feel, not even their children. An elder needs to realize that the changes occurring in his or her life are bringing changes to the child's life as well. In fact, telling your parent about the concern and need to help that has entered your life through their illness or disability can open up a way to improve their self esteem through helping them realize their importance to you.

However, be cautious when using generalities about common responses to illness and disability. Remember that many differences exist within the elderly population. Consider, for example, the fact that competition and comparison can be strong motivating factors to help certain people improve their health but may provide barriers to others. Competition and comparison are likely to be huge obstacles in motivating the elderly, particularly women. Successful women in the 2000's are likely to say that they only compete with themselves. Their mothers are more likely to compete with every woman they meet. Comparisons are usually made by comparing the elder's worst features with the best features of the object of their comparison. Here are a few examples from my clients:

♦ "I could never be like her; she's a Smith graduate, and I didn't finish high school."

♦ "Well, of course, she looks pretty! Look at that beautiful skin – why, it's 'Georgia peach.' My acne scars have shown all my life."

♦ "She raised three perfect kids, at least it sounds like it. I only had one, and I ruined him."

The common denominator in such unfavorable comparisons is low self esteem.

Each generation learns certain norms about wellness vs. illness. Each generation faces different health challenges in spite of some that have remained fairly consistent across generations, such as infections and arthritis. Parents can help their adult children understand their reactions to illness and disability without behaving as if the stances they take are immutable. In fact, parents need their children to understand, even though admitting and examining their fears has probably not been a norm of the elder's generation. In Western culture, many of today's elders were taught that illness and decline are inevitable. Some 90 year-olds still believe the only reason they will be hospitalized is because they are dying.

On the other hand, if you are a 'baby boomer,' you are likely to have been raised on self-help literature, given a lot of information about preventive health, and taught to be self-assertive from birth. Your generation tends to respond to health problems with "How soon can you fix it?" The 'take charge' attitude attributed to the 'boomers' by Ken Dychtwald and others who have studied them can be very helpful to your parents. At the same time, you and your parents need to learn to communicate compassionately about your differences. Communication skills and exercises like those in the next chapter can help both groups achieve more clarity with each other.

Climate of Acceptance

Approaching the challenges posed by illness or disability should occur in the context of a climate of acceptance. The story of Walter and Eloise is a concrete example of how an emotional climate of acceptance, patience, and love is necessary to produce healthy changes in people's lives. It was energizing to continue my work with Eloise and Walter as they took another Inventory, this time of their strengths as a couple.

With their strengths Inventory accomplished, the three of us worked together on re-Structuring their lives to reflect a healthier dependence/independence balance. When their plan for the new Structure of their lives was in place, we enjoyed brain-storming about creative choices they could make to accomplish the goals of the Structure they wanted. We also brain-stormed Choices they could make toward moving from their "stuck" selves into their *selves-in-becoming.*

Walter and Eloise are examples of finding a balanced perspective. Walter lived out his life with Parkinson's. Eloise lived until his death as the wife of a man who suffered from Parkinson's Disease. It was the way they chose to live it out, the choices they made about their relationship, and the effect of viewing themselves as whole persons that made the difference! Aging well means looking squarely at the reality of the situation, facing the feelings, beliefs, and problems the reality brings into your lives, and Choosing to <u>live</u> as you deal with it!

Just as Walter and Eloise needed to understand each other's experience of Walter's Parkinson's disease, adult children and their parents need to understand each other's beliefs about health and illness. Respect for each other's different perspectives is an important factor in building your climate of acceptance. There has been perhaps too much emphasis on the 'generation gap.' Naturally, each generation has its own history, its own norms, and its own ways of relating to the world. Nonetheless, intergenerational projects like foster grandparent programs are increasingly demonstrating that bridges can be built across 'gaps' in generations by building a climate of acceptance. Each generation has valuable information to share with others, and each can benefit from mutual exchange.

It is important to remember that no person is ever simply an illness ("I am a cancer patient.") or a disability ("I am an amputee."). The individual who has a diagnosed illness and/or disability must be viewed through a holistic lens that shows the whole person – body, mind, and soul. Acceptance of oneself as a whole person who is dealing with an illness or disability is a part of the climate of acceptance. I encourage my clients to refer to themselves with sentences like "I am an elementary school teacher who has three children, a husband, a cat, and diabetes." This is an example of how I use cognitive restructuring with my clients, a technique explained in the next chapter. It is a method that is far deeper than simply using different words to encourage denial or a 'Pollyanna' attitude. It actually reinforces an empowered, healthy approach that is conducive to health and wellness.

As you and your elders continue to build your climate of acceptance, you need to spend time thinking and talking about what makes life meaningful for you and for your elders. One of the most significant aspects of guiding elders and their loved ones through the journey is helping the elders identify and articulate their lives in terms of what Mary Baird Carlsen calls "meaning-making." Carlsen's work on "developmental meaning-making theory" was used in developing the framework of this guide. I relied upon it strongly because it is congruent with what my clients taught me. The values we hold, the world view in which we believe, and what is meaningful to us are inextricably woven into the fabric of our lives.

If you choose to change your life it may necessitate reviewing and changing your world view to bring it more into accord with your values. It could denote exchanging a relationship that has become meaningless for a relationship in which you can give and receive nurturance, support, and love. Doing so does not imply changing the person with whom you are relating. It indicates changing the nature of the relationship from a meaningless one to one that has meaning for you and the other(s) in it.

Chapter 4: Communicating Clearly & Compassionately

"Authentic relationships are, for me,
the oxygen for the breath of survival."
The Author

This chapter will explore the role of communication in adult-to-adult relationships and give examples of how more effective communication can improve relationships. Communication is an integral part of our relatedness to others. Clear, considerate, and authentic communication fosters an understanding relationship. Guidelines and specific exercises for working through *RISC* are included. Specific exercises are given to help you communicate effectively as you explore each of the territories involved in the journey from relating adult to adult to facing the end of the journey.

Becoming more effective in communication involves skills and practice. It also involves understanding that communication is more than just a tool. The term 'communication' embraces numerous components, including: a) nonverbal behavior b) listening skills c) choice of words d) timing of the exchange e) attitudes of persons attempting to communicate and f) feedback. Our discussion of effective communication focuses on its use in adult-to-adult sharing of the journey into aging. Therefore, when the term 'effective communication' is used in this book, it means communication that:

+ takes place within a climate of acceptance
+ is clear and authentic
+ is compassionate and caring
+ enhances growth in relationships
+ facilitates doing the work in *RISC*
+ reinforces positive attitudes that support healthy aging
+ involves risks associated with changing communication patterns and styles

Styles of communication vary greatly depending upon a family's culture and its characteristics. Norms develop within a given family for appropriate behavior regarding exchange of feelings, thoughts, attitudes, and opinions. What might seem intrusive in one family could be a sign of caring in another. In one family, a lack of verbal communication may lead to misunderstandings, while in another, there may be plenty of warm communication without many words. But sometimes there is a communication pattern that seriously interferes with actually being in a true relationship. In that event, it is worthwhile to try to find out what is being cloaked by the pattern.

Perhaps you and your elder, spouse, or friend have a set pattern for what you say to each other partly because you find a certain amount of security in that ritual. It could be that you and the other adult have adopted this communication pattern as a way of staving off real communication. Here are some guidelines for improving communication that have been developed from personal and professional experience.

Guidelines for Improving Communication

In general, communication that enhances healthy adult-to-adult relationships is clear, focused, authentic, compassionate, caring, kind, and considerate. Guidelines and general knowledge about communication comprise entire books, and many such books are available. One popular topic concerns gender differences in communication. Deborah Tannen's <u>You Just Don't Understand</u>, and John Grey's <u>Men Are From Mars, Women Are From Venus</u> are examples of books that explore gender differences.

There are also common generational, educational, and cultural communication differences to learn about and consider. The guidelines listed below were derived from my study of the communication difficulties that most frequently surfaced with my clients, but they pertain to communication among all adults. Many of them were derived from working with colleagues, siblings and friends. As you read through them, think about communications in your relationships that contribute to hurt feelings, 'stalemates,' or misunderstandings. You can begin to improve them by paying attention to the guidelines.

Clarity, Focus, and Authenticity

- ◆ Pay attention to whether you are being congruent – that is, do your body language, facial expression, tone of voice, and choice of words convey the same message? A statement like "It doesn't matter," delivered in an irritable tone with a facial expression of frustration, hurt, or anger, is NOT a congruent message.

♦ Think how you can restructure statements so that they are 'I' rather than 'you' messages. Stating what you 'own' is your role. Listening carefully to what the other 'owns' is done by giving them the opportunity to make 'I' statements about themselves.

♦ Try to be willing to 'own' your feelings about a communication. Use openings such as, "It embarrasses me to say this, but...;" "This is hard to bring up...;" and "I don't find this easy to talk about..."

♦ Keep dialogue open by using reflections and open-ended statements, for example., "sounds like you have some thoughts about that;" "I hope you can say how you feel about this;" and "your opinion is ...?"

♦ Be open about what you believe you do/do not understand. A dialogue is not a debate or a contest. Use clear messages such as "I'm not clear what your last statement is about;" "Can you help me understand your basic point?" or "I'd like to put what you said in my own words. Please let me know if this is accurate."

♦ Keep in mind that effective communication involves dialogue, and that means being able to listen attentively as well as speak clearly. If you are formulating your next words while the other is speaking, you are not listening attentively.

Compassion and Caring

- ◆ Refrain from speaking in anger, if at all possible. If you do speak in anger, plan with your elder or other adult for a specific time to return to the topic when you feel less angry. The role of anger in communication patterns is discussed later in the chapter.
- ◆ Try to refrain from making judgmental or accusatory statements. Accusatory statements often begin with "you" followed by "always" or "never." Such remarks elicit defensive retorts rather than responsive dialogue.
- ◆ Communication can be compassionate even when agreement cannot be reached. If another adult states beliefs or ideas with which you cannot authentically agree, there is still 'room' to relate. Saying something like, "I respect your belief, while I cannot at this time say I share it," leaves space in the relationship that would be shut down by saying something like, "You're wrong!"
- ◆ Communication is, at best, imperfect. When you recognize a word choice or way of communication that conveys less compassion and clarity than you wish, correct it. For example, if you become aware your body is turning away, change your posture. If you say, "you can't" when "I wish you would not" is more compassionate, correct with something like, "I said 'can't' when what I would rather convey to you is that I wish you would not. As an adult, of course you can, but may we discuss it?"

Kindness and Consideration

♦ Avoid labels, i.e., 'wrong;' 'dumb;' 'silly.' Labels block communication and distort it with subjective notions about what the labels mean. This also applies to avoiding labels for yourself, such as, "that was a stupid question I asked."

♦ Avoid giving direct advice or directions unless specifically requested by the other – and even then, be careful! Be alert to messages that include words like 'should,' 'ought,' and 'cannot.' Suggesting and requesting are effective ways of addressing another adult – not ordering.

♦ Think before you answer. Quick retorts seldom send a message to which another can respond positively. Also, they may send a message you do not actually want to deliver. You have probably had the experience of giving a quick, "sure, I'll do it" response to a request you do something, later regretting your rapid acquiescence.

♦ Choose words that enhance growth rather than indicating lack of confidence in the other's ability. "I believe when you think this through you can…" is more conducive to growth than "Let me tell you what I think you should do."

♦ Be aware of your body language. Such behavior as turning away from the other person, standing up and rocking back and forth on your heels, and drumming your fingers are typically signs that you wish communication to cease. Something about it is making you uncomfortable – it may be impatience, disagreement, anger, judgment, preoccupation with being elsewhere, indifference to the other, or some other barrier to communication. Overcoming barriers to communication will be discussed later in the chapter.

Stress Reduction and Communication

The more at ease we are, the more likely we can communicate clearly and compassionately. The importance of reducing stress is mentioned throughout the book. Stress reduction has many benefits, and achieving more effective communication is only one of them. Some others are: a) physiological benefits such as lowering blood pressure and improving breathing, b) cognitive benefits such as improving concentration and increasing mental focus, c) psychological benefits such as lowering anxiety, and d) spiritual benefits such as inner peace.

Here are some ways to reduce stress that you can try as you work with this book and in numerous ways as you choose. I include them here because when I teach people how to communicate more effectively, I include stress reduction as an integral part of that experience. The list is not prioritized. That part is up to you.

- Inducing the Relaxation Response as described by Dr. Herbert Benson
- Meditation
- Prayer
- Imagery – solitary imaging, guided imagery, or both
- Physical exercise
- Massage
- Yoga

- Laughing - use humor to 'lighten up'
- Relaxation exercises such as Jacobson's pro-gressive relaxation
- Relaxing in water, such as hot tubs, jaccuzi, swimming, herbal baths
- Slowly sipping decaffeinated herbal teas or coffee, fruit juices, or water
- Listening to calming music

Monitoring Your Inner Dialogue

A common saying when I grew up was "sticks and stones may break my bones, but words can never hurt me." WRONG! The words we use to describe ourselves, our circumstances, and others have a powerful effect on the way we feel about them. Ultimately, they have a strong effect on our beliefs about them. For example, think about the words that 'play' in your mind as you think about yourself. If words like 'stupid,' or phrases that suggest inadequacy, like "there you go again, dummy" reoccur in our minds over time, we will eventually believe them about ourselves.

It is important to pay attention to the way we communicate internally, which is what I am calling our inner dialogue. I am not suggesting you moni-tor your inner dialogue so compulsively that you become anxious about trying to control it. This is a matter of becoming attentive, or 'listening' actively to yourself, in much the same manner you listen attentively to another person. It involves being compassionate, kind, and considerate of yourself as well as others. I suggest you try re-framing your inner dialogue along with trying the stress reduc-tion techniques listed above.

Cognitive restructuring, or re-framing, literally substitutes one set of descriptors for another in our minds. The process is more complex than this way of stating it, but this is a helpful way to begin to understand it. Those of you who are familiar with neurolinguistic programming and other sophisticated methods of cognitive behavioral psychology will recognize at once how I am oversimplifying the concepts involved. My experience shows that an effective way to help people become willing to try changing their thoughts is to de-mystify the subject. You will find references for this chapter that can help you delve more deeply into the topic if you wish.

People who specialize in motivational behavioral skills, for example, Steven Covey, use a variety of techniques that encourage re-framing. Changing the thoughts that hurt us facilitates not only more effective communication but also improved self-esteem. I am often asked, "Isn't this just a new 'spin' on 'the power of positive thinking?' " The answer is both yes and no. Simply calling something by a different word will not change reality. Cognitive restructuring, or re-framing, goes deeper than that. Nonetheless, I encourage you to remember the value of 'baby steps' as you learn to change the behavior you want to change.

When we are children, we internalize words that adults use to describe us and others. Internalized 'messages' about who we are may be interfering with the effectiveness of our communication. The value of re-framing extends far beyond its contribution to communication. It is applicable to psychotherapy and to many aspects of mental health. It is placed here because our ability to use it skillfully in communication influences our ability to apply it to more complex aspects of our lives.

Adult-to-Adult Communication Between Younger and Older People

Ask yourself whether you are treating the elder as you would treat other adults at your office, in your organizations, when doing business, or in the homes of your friends. A parent-child relationship is different than the examples above, but using that 'check' can be helpful to you in evaluating your communication with elders. Differences in communication styles are to be expected. However, sometimes there is so much frustration, confusion, anxiety or anger involved in a relationship with a parent that attention to those feelings must precede meaningful changes in communication patterns.

Overall, communication with an elder becomes more effective when you have better understanding of what may be contributing to the elder's behavior. Let's think about some situations involving elders that surface repeatedly in my experience. If you are an elder reading this, allow your self to take the risk of **R**ecognizing yourself in these examples. Keep in mind that **R**ecognition is the first step in the *RISC* process.

We all know an elder who talks constantly, or who repeats the same stock stories to anyone who will listen. There could be a number of reasons, and a compassionate approach would be to try to discern what is underlying seemingly compulsive talking or repeating. It may be the parent has a cognitive dysfunction and really doesn't know that she or he is telling the same story repeatedly. To check this out, you may ask something like, "Mom, have you told me this story before?" If she doesn't know she has, refer back to the information in Chapter 3 about obtaining a good geriatric health assessment. If she says she has told you but expresses a desire to repeat it often, encourage her to express the meaning of the story to her or to explore how she finds it comforting to repeat it.

Sometimes learning what the emotional meaning of a story is to the elder helps you increase your tolerance for hearing it again. It may provide ways to enrich your communication by asking about different aspects of the story. You may also look for resources in your community that would give her additional outlets to tell her story, such as reminiscence or story-telling groups at senior centers.

Elders sometimes repeat the same statements or questions over and over because what they really seek is a more empathic response. Jane was an 83 year-old woman who repeatedly said to her daughters, "You know I am a sick woman," in response to numerous situations. As Jane and I explored her frequent statement we discovered it was "code" for her unexplored and unexpressed fears of dying. When Jane and I talked together with her daughters about her fears about dying and made some plans to help her with them, she no longer felt the need to remind them "You know I am a sick woman."

In a different elder's life, that same statement could have an entirely different meaning. For example, it could be an indirect way of stating, "I need more attention." It could be a manipulative way of saying, "I want you to spend more time with me;" a plea for understanding how much pain and suffering the elder is experiencing; or any number of other messages depending on the people involved.

Repetitive stories and/or statements are sometimes ruses to avoid direct communication, though not necessarily consciously recognized as such. Elders who are aware they are experiencing mild memory lapses often 'cover up' the gaps in conversation by reverting to familiar stories or phrases. If you notice the elder responding to a variety of situations and conversations with the same thing, it would be well to consider your observation in the context of the elder's overall health. If this repetitive story telling is a recent pattern, you may want to investigate whether the elder is depressed. When people are depressed they have poverty of thought. These may be the only thoughts that are occurring to him or her.

Some people spend more time reminiscing or reviewing their life experience as they age. Very often they are satisfied with their lives and even more tolerant of themselves than they were at a younger age. Re-living life experiences may bring them satisfaction and pleasant memories to be re-experienced. On the other hand, there are memories that trigger guilt about how well they have functioned, for example, as parents. An elder may become a prisoner of this process and obsess over mistakes she has made. Instead of being expressed directly, those regrets may become camouflaged. It is hard to step back and view communication patterns dispassionately, but we can learn a lot about ourselves and the elder just by listening to what is said. A truly adult response like "I notice you tell that over and over," will be more effective than one like "You told me that! You're getting on my nerves repeating it!"

If you hear the elder saying repeatedly, "I'm sorry," or "Don't get mad at me but," or "I'm no good at anything anymore," or "Nothing I do is right," then it is logical to ask what she is so sorry about. Another manifestation of guilt is projecting the blame onto you through statements such as, "You never like anything I wear," or "I can't do anything right as far as you're concerned." Actions may also communicate that the elder is struggling with guilt feelings. Being overly solicitous, agreeing with everything you say, waiting on you, or buying you items you don't want or need may be ways of atoning for guilt without really confronting it directly and resolving it. Elders, of course, do not have a monopoly on guilt. You may recognize that you or others display the same behaviors that signal guilt in the elder.

You and the elder need to pay close attention to choices of words, feelings, and old communication habits as you both seek to become more truly adult in communicating with one another. After all, you have your lifetime of past habits, word choices, and patterns influencing your current relationships – a lot of old 'baggage' to unload before you can be truly adult in your communication. I've heard elders say to their adult children, "You should be ashamed of yourself." Moralistic, shaming comments can be very hurtful and abort your efforts to be truly adult in your relationship. Judgmental comments, such as, "Oh, Dad, stop that! You know it irritates me" exemplify ways of communication that are more akin to pouting adolescence than to truly adult ways of relating to an elder. It helps to be patient with yourself and your elders and to remember that ways of communicating took years to develop and will not be replaced overnight.

It is healthy to keep in mind that you can be responsible for only one person's feelings and behavior – your own. What you say can reflect this. There is a world of difference between, "You never listen to what I say," and "I feel that you may not be hearing what I just said." The former shuts down reception; the latter may open up the channel of communication. Even if you can change only what you say and do, your changes are likely to bring about different responses eventually.

Once more effective patterns emerge, they are likely to be rewarding in themselves. Think about how much easier it is to hear, "we can talk about that," than to hear "the subject is closed." Even if you and the elder agree to suspend a subject because of inability to resolve differences, or **Recog**nize it is inflicting pain, think about the difference between "all right; we will agree to put that topic in the freezer for now," and "Stop, I don't want to hear another word about it."

Overcoming Barriers to Compassionate Communication

The parties in a compassionate relationship know that it matters how they talk to each other. However, human relationships being what they are, people feel hurt from time to time even in a compassionate and understanding relationship. However, good communication reduces the number and degree of hurts and misunderstandings. As a relationship grows, and as people become more effectively involved with each other, they each become more understanding about how the other communicates, both verbally and nonverbally.

Time itself can become a barrier, however. Unresolved issues in the relationship that have been pushed below the surface of awareness over and over for years are likely to become more deeply 'buried' and to increase over time. Couples who have been married for many years are sometimes appalled at the harsh words, actions, or feelings that seem to erupt 'out of nowhere,' like a volcanic explosion in their marriage. Often such feelings appear out of proportion to anything current in the relationship, thereby adding a sense of their being unjustified to the shock of feeling out of control when they erupt.

The sooner adults in relationship recognize issues between them and make plans to manage them, the more likely they are to be capable of compassion toward one another. Spouses of many years sometimes 'brag' to me that , "We have never had a fight;" or "Not a harsh word has ever passed between us." As a psychotherapist, when I hear such assertions, I can only pray they will have help to survive the explosion if they live long enough for it to happen. As a holistic health care provider, I look at their health challenges – such as elevated blood pressure, ulcers, headaches, and eating disorders with clearer awareness of the dynamics involved.

Anger interferes with communication. If you allow yourself to 'vent' your anger, you will say or do something both you and your adult in relationship may regret later. If you 'swallow' your anger

146 Aging as a Shared Journey

and fail to address it in a constructive way, it is likely to appear in your relationship in disguise – unexplained silent treatments, forgetting, sabotaging, resentment, rejection, withdrawal, punishing, or other signs of lack of compassion.

When anger erupts, it is a good idea to take a 'cooling off' period, but not one that is so long it drives the anger 'underground.' If your anger needs help to dissipate, using some form of displacement like brisk physical exercise, hitting a pillow, or shredding paper with your hands is a good idea. Before it subsides entirely, I recommend writing it out with no effort to censor – just write whatever comes to mind on paper you can destroy easily if you choose to do that later.

Anger-in-writing (or drawing) can be an effective tool in planning ways to manage your anger compassionately. Sometimes, something will emerge when you review it at a later time that helps you use humor as a healthy coping device to deal with anger. Whenever you feel more calm, look for themes – are there hints of things you have been angry about in the relationship for a long time? Are there things that surprise you, that you thought weren't bothering you? Make a list of what you need to talk about with your loved one. Give yourself permission to tackle the list in small steps. Make an appointment with your loved one to spend an exact amount of time beginning on your list.

Compassion may be impeded by fear or anxiety about communication. One of my clients, Jim, had been in therapy for treatment of depression about six weeks. In one of his sessions, Jim recalled a time in the early days of his marriage when his wife, Sue, had threatened to leave him if he ever mentioned a certain previous girlfriend of his again. Now, forty years later, the former 'girlfriend' died and Jim became angry when his wife suggested they attend her funeral. "Oh, just shut up about it!" he shouted at his wife. Failing to understand Jim's response, Sue continued to plan to attend the funeral. As she did so, Jim's shouting continued and his responses became increasingly hostile. Surprised by his outburst, Jim brought the issue to therapy.

Jim discovered he was grieving that he had never taken the opportunity to become friends with his former girlfriend and the man she married, or given them the opportunity to get to know him and his wife and children. Jim's harshness toward his wife was behavior that puzzled them both until he was able to recognize that his fear of telling her about his regrets was fueling his lack of compassionate communication with her. While Jim's fear may have been out of proportion to the situation, it was actually fear of losing his wife that had originally blocked his ability to communicate his feelings to her compassionately.

More often, the fear is the vague, uneasy, unexplored feeling we call anxiety. I encourage you to explore possibilities for more compassionate communication with your loved ones by being willing to explore your anxieties about 'what if' and 'what could happen' in your relationships.

Alfred Hitchcock made an international reputation as a film director and probably a great deal of money by recognizing the truth that humans can cause themselves more anxiety by their imaginings than reality can cause them. As uncomfortable as

anxiety is, it likely to yield to compassionate communication. Some examples are:

- ◆ "I know this is hard for you, but I will stay
  with you while we work it out."
- ◆ "I get anxious when we begin on this subject,
  but I am willing to stay with it until we help
  one another feel more comfortable with it."
- ◆ "Let's begin by becoming still and breathing
  together quietly for a little while until one of
  us feels comfortable enough to begin talking
  about this."
- ◆ "I believe we both feel anxious about this. I
  also believe if we discuss it together and
  share our anxious thoughts we can help one
  another work it out peacefully."
- ◆ "I understand you may not feel as anxious as
  I do, but please bear with me while I tell you
  about this." Or – "I am not aware of feeling
  anxious about this, but I want to listen while
  you tell me about your anxious feelings."

Communication Skills Needed for Working through RISC

As you use the steps, **R**ecognition; **I**nventorying; **S**tructuring; and **C**hoosing more and more,
you will discover communication skills that work
well for you; favorite ones you will rely on; and
new ones you can write to me about so I can add
them to my next book! Here are some examples to
get you started:

Recognition
Think about an uncomfortable communication
pattern with the elder or other important adult in

your life that recurs in your experience. It does not have to be a BIG one. Even small irritations that accompany repetitive patterns can become larger aggravations over time. Visualize this pattern, bringing it into your mind's eye as accurately as you can. Answer for yourself the following questions about it (make notes):

    a. What is my body language telling me?
    b. What is her/his body language telling me?
    c. What is the major feeling I have in this scene?
    d. What happens every time this scene happens?
    e. What do I fear will happen if I change my behavior?
    f. What about this scene tells me something needs changing?
    g. Do I blame myself for this scene, or the other adult, or both of us?

Inventorying

Make a list of the resources you and the elder have to deal with to communicate more compassionately with one another. A list is a communication to yourself. It is also a device you can use to communicate to the elder or with other adults you may have in mind. Save it to remind you of the strengths you and your elder bring to the situation you wish to improve. Be sure to include communication skills you have now and also ones you can learn.

Structuring

Make an appointment with the adult you are doing this exercise with to plan the time you will give to beginning to structure your more effective communication. If the change appears to be relatively minor, less time will need to be planned. Nonetheless, be open to the possibility that compassionate communication may lead to discovery of something more important than it initially appears. Below is an example of how this worked for Emily and Ruth, whom you met in Chapter 2.

Emily and her mother, Ruth, made an inventory that included their mutual interest in the theater and movies as a source of enjoyment they could share. Emily called Ruth to make an appointment to explore the topic further so they could add related activities to their new structure for being in relationship. They met at a favorite restaurant, agreeing to spend one hour on the topic of entertainment. Their conversation went something like this:

Emily: "Well, Mom, I can tell you right off that scary movies and violence are out for me. I have nightmares afterwards, and so I don't consider them entertainment."

Ruth: "When you were a little girl, you were a scary-cat. I never could figure out why you frightened so easily."

Emily: "Mom, this is supposed to be dialogue – not therapy. Be my mother, please."

Ruth: "Oh, I've got to get the hang of this. All right; I agree about violence, so we can rule out violent movies or plays. We won't consider them entertainment. Still, I enjoy suspense and a little titillating scary stuff."

Emily: "Mom, you're supposed to be more careful about your heart. You might get it racing by watching that scary stuff; it wouldn't be good for you."

Ruth: "Emily, this is supposed to be mutual – not parental. Please be my daughter, not my mother."

Emily: "Agreed. Do you enjoy romantic movies,

even the ones about youngsters in love for
the first time?"

Ruth: "Oh, yes, young love – old love – all ro-
mance appeals to me."

Emily: "What about the classic love stories in
plays, such as, "Romeo and Juliet," or
'Othello" now there's a deep one!"

Ruth: "They're OK but I would rather get into
some new works I'm not familiar with. We
both love to read. Why don't we decide on a
book neither of us has read – a romantic one
– and then see the play or the movie?"

Emily: "I like that. As we do more of this,
though, I want to understand your enjoyment
of scary stuff better. And I'd like you to
understand my anxiety about it better. We'll
need to build some ways into our structure
to deal with that if we agree to do it."

Ruth: "I've got it! We'll wait 'til this feels more
natural to us. Then we'll agree on a scary
movie; go see it; then schedule a therapy
session with Monteen to process our responses to the movie."

And they did! You're beginning to see how this
works, aren't you? The best way is to try it out in
your own life experience.

Choosing

As I've said earlier, **Choosing** how you will
change becomes a dynamic, ever evolving process
that provides new aspects of life to recognize,
inventory, structure, and choose. Here are some
examples of the difference between communication
that supports **Choosing** and communication that
supports passively letting life 'happen to you.'

a. "I see 3 possibilities here. The last one appeals most to me overall, so it is what I choose to do." vs. "Three possibilities are too many; pick one for me."

b. "I have decided to wait until I get more information before I choose. Choosing to wait is also a choice." vs. "I don't know. I can't tell what to do."

c. "The consequences of this choice are ones I can live with, so it's my choice." vs. "Everything has consequences. What do you want me to do?"

d. "This choice is my preference for now. As circumstances change, I reserve the right to change it." vs. "What if I choose this and regret it later?"

e. "I did that, and now, with hindsight, I can see another action might have been better. Now that I have more information, I will forgive myself for that decision and proceed with one I now think is better." vs. "How could I ever have let myself make that stupid decision? Now look at the mess I'm in!"

As you can see, thousands of examples like the above are possible. As you become conscious of expressing yourself and listening to your loved ones with this kind of differentiation in mind, you can be more compassionate toward yourself and others. You can approach life experiences with a healthy, proactive stance.

Communication Exercises to Build Your Skills for the Journey

Congratulations on being a pioneer in exploring the relatively uncharted territory of Aging as a Shared Journey. We are working with a basic map and exploring the terrain as we go along. You were given directions for your first bold exercise in heartwork in Chapter 1. We will continue here with more exercises to help you build your skills. Each one relates to a different chapter, or 'territory.' Try them more than once as your confidence and your understanding of the guide grow. You will use them in different ways as your journey evolves.

Relating Adult-to-Adult Exercise

It is common to feel 'silly' when doing this exercise, but the shared humor about it tends to build strength in your relationship. I recommend you do this exercise with an observer adult coaching you especially when you are beginners at this. It is easier to become frustrated than you might think, but it is definitely worth the effort! Here's how to do it:

1. Pick a topic you wish to discuss with the elder, another adult who is doing this exercise with you. Ask the person you pick if she is willing to try this with you.
2. Ask a third adult to be your 'coach' in a dialogue between the two of you. You may ask your counselor, therapist, minister, teacher, or any relatively 'uninvolved party.' In other words, your third adult should be able to be objective. We will call this third adult the 'coach.'

3. When the two of you agree on a time and place for your dialogue, make arrangements for the 'coach' adult to meet you there. Provide the coach with a bell, a whistle, or any sound-making object you can tolerate. As you dialogue, the coach should make the sound each and every time one of you says, does, or shows by appearance anything that is not characteristic of equal adults in dialogue. This means all communication between the two of you must be respectful and implies that any behavior less than adult will be 'called.' When the sound interrupts you, the behavior must be corrected.

A variation on this exercise is to videotape your dialogue and critique it yourselves by stopping the video and correcting each and every time one of you spots a behavior that is not respectful, egalitarian behavior.

Meeting the Challenges of Aging and Illness Exercise

This is a variation of an exercise I used in "Aging and Mental Health" classes with graduate students. You and an adult partner will take turns doing this one. I suggest you draw straws or flip a coin to decide which one becomes 'disabled' first.

Here's how to proceed:
1. Put soap on one lens of a pair of glasses so you cannot see through it and enough on the other lens to make seeing 'hazy.' Then the one taking the healthier role does the following:
2. Put the glasses on the 'disabled' one.
3. Use gauze or yarn or some similar fabric to

tie her dominant arm to her side just se-
curely enough to restrict movement (do not
cut off circulation!).

4. Put shoes on his feet that are at least two
   sizes too large, so that walking
   will be more difficult.
5. Be the helping adult while you walk around,
   preferably outdoors, at least
   five minutes.
6. Go back inside and help the 'disabled' one
   enjoy a good, nutritious snack,
   for example, a cup of tea, a piece of fruit, and
   some cookies.
7. Reverse the roles and do the exercise with
   the other before you discuss
   anything about the experience.

When both of you have completed the exercise,
talk about how it felt, what thoughts went through
your minds as you did it, and anything pertinent to
the experience that occurs to you. Be very specific,
for example, "You let crumbs fall on my neck when
you put that cookie in my mouth;" or "I thought
you had just left me there and gone back inside."

Compassionate Communication Exercise

Life is full of interesting moments. This is one!
I love to get letters telling me about what experiences people have when they do this exercise. It is
so like life – filled with potential and always dynamic! Here it is:

1. When you are together with an elder or another adult you choose to share the exercise,
   set a timer to ring at the end of 30 minutes.
   One of you just begin talking about some-

thing that you feel strongly about – do not
agree ahead of time on what you will talk
about – just start talking about something,
somewhere in the midst of your thought,
feelings, and concerns. Take turns doing the
same kind of talking, being sure you are
talking about something that is truly meaningful to you and that you feel passionately
about – do not concern yourself with how the
other adult might think or feel about it OR
with the two of you talking about the same
thing. Think in terms of each of you having
about one-half the time to talk, but do not
concern yourself during this part with keeping time. When the 30-minute reminder
rings, note whether you feel you got equal
opportunity to talk. Store that information
in your memory for future reflection on the
nature of the communication between you
and the person who shared the exercise with
you.

2. When the timer rings, stop and reset the
timer for 20 minutes, without saying a word.
Each of you write whatever comes to you
separately for 20 minutes. Still without saying a word, exchange your written notes.

3. Set the timer for 10 minutes, still without
exchanging words Each of you read what the
other wrote, without talking.

4. When the timer rings, stop reading; face one
another; look each other directly in the eyes,
and do whatever feels right. Call your
mother; fight and cry over the experience;
separate in silence; contact your therapist;
go out to dinner – whatever authentically
feels right.

5. If the two of you do not 'fall into' doing what-

ever feels right together, go your separate
ways and arrange a later time to talk through
the experience with one another and who-
ever else you need to involve.
6. Do not allow more than two days to go by
before you get together to talk it over.

Resolving Unfinished Business Exercise

This exercise can be done alone, or you and
other adults can do it together and then talk about
how it felt afterward. We did this one in classes for
nursing students, and the ensuing conversations
about how it felt were always stimulating and rewarding. Occasionally, someone feels strong feelings of sadness or regret, or some other extreme
emotion in relation to this exercise. If you experience such strength of emotion that you are uncomfortable while you are doing it, stop until you can
do it with someone who can comfort you. If you
experience such strong emotion after you do the
exercise, seek an understanding adult friend, pas-
tor, counselor, or health care professional and
discuss the effect you experienced from doing it.
Go ahead and try it:

1. Pick a time when you can be uninterrupted
for a minimum of 30 minutes. Place two 8 x
11 sheets of blank paper and a pen in front
of you. Sit in a relaxed position to write, and
allow yourself to become relaxed. When you
feel calm, set the timer for 20 -25 minutes.
2. Write a letter to a loved one as if it will be the
last thing you will do before you die. "Pre-
tend" you will never have the opportunity to
speak with your loved one in this life, and
write your loved one what is uppermost in

your mind – your last words to her or him.

3. When the timer rings, sit back and relax. Allow yourself to recognize you have done a communication exercise and that it is in your power to destroy, keep, or handle what you wrote in any way you choose.

4. Next, re-read what you have written. Answer for yourself the following questions:
   a. "Did I write about something I regret?"
   b. "Is there something here I need to straighten out (forgive; clarify; explain; ask for) with regard to the person to whom I wrote?"
   c. "Are there any surprises here for me?"
   d. "What could I do to actually take care of this unfinished business?"

5. Decide whether to keep or destroy your letter. This is an individual choice decision. There are no 'right' and 'wrong' ways to do it. If you decide to keep your letter, you may want to share it with the person to whom you wrote it someday; but whether or not you do is entirely up to you – again, no 'right' or 'wrong' choice. Also, if you decide to keep it, it remains your own, and a later decision to destroy it can be made any time.

I once discovered one of these I had written and forgotten I'd kept lying inside one of my journals. It was synchronicity – I discovered it the very week I regained communication with the person to whom I had written it. That discovery was most helpful to me in deciding how I wanted to manage my participation in the opportunity to reconnect with that relationship!

This is an exercise I find so helpful that I have done it many times, and I will surely do it again. It helps me keep in touch with what is working and what needs to be worked out in my life. And there is always plenty of both.

Facing the End of the Journey Exercise

This is a piece of cake! Write your obituary. I'M SERIOUS. Sit down right now, put the book down, and write your obituary. If your experience is anything like mine or my clients', you will regularly write it, tear it up, and rewrite it. It works like life works. It is continuous, ongoing, changing, and a work-in-progress until the final word is written and the final breath is taken.

I have had the wonderfully rewarding experience of relating with many clients who made contracts in which they committed to LIVE until they died. Those contracts involved listing unfinished business they planned to finish, but they also involved discoursing, discussing, praying, and writing about how they experienced imminent dying. Out of those experiences, I am convinced that the healthiest way to LIVE is to conceptualize each of our days as potentially our last one on this earth. Keeping 'living one day at a time' in mind is not the same thing as being morbid. Rather, it emphasizes **R**ecognizing how much we can enjoy, being grateful for small things, and being alert to beauty in everyday life.

You may wish to write your obituary in the same form they appear in the newspaper, including names, birth date, and other biographical information. One of my students wrote a five-page obituary (he was 43 – wonder what his obituary looks like today?). I do mine so often that I tend to make them short, though that is no way more correct than any other. If I write another book, you will probably see a different obituary. Here is mine for today:

She followed her heart.

She loved, and was loved by, many dear stardust companions.

It mattered that she did live.

She is grateful for her life and the lives of those to whom she gave birth.

She died knowing she was going home to God!

There are endless possibilities for communication exercises to help us keep in touch with ourselves, our loved ones, and our lives. There are endless possibilities for communication exercises to help us more clearly communicate what our hearts hold and to help us be more compassionate in our communications. The pivotal understanding is to comprehend that it is vital that we learn ways to communicate our authentic selves to one another. Our relationships, and ultimately the quality of our lives, will be embedded in our ways of communicating with one another. Life presents us with many opportunities to increase our compassionate response to it – to be more compassionate to ourselves, and to others.

Chapter 5: Resolving Unfinished Business

"When thou dost ask me blessing, I'll kneel down,
And ask of thee forgiveness: so we'll live,
And pray, and sing, and tell old tales, and laugh..."
William Shakespeare

By now, you probably have an increasingly clear picture of how the term 'mental health' is used to refer to wholeness, as well as how it applies to healthy aging. Being mentally healthy implies working out the developmental tasks of life successfully, adapting to life's changing circumstances in constructive and life-affirming ways, and engaging in lifelong learning and growing. As you increase effective ways to maintain and improve your mental health, the rewards of sharing your journey into aging will expand. You and your fellow travelers will grow in relationship as you share authentically what aging means for you.

As a pathfinder to help you with your journey, I ask you to recognize past experiences that may not be resolved in your life. Unresolved issues, or unfinished business, may or may not be influencing your life currently; but it is important to consider the possibility. In this chapter, a few of the numerous examples of clients who have profited by resolving unfinished business are included.

In 1979, I began focusing much of my psychotherapy practice on people who had life-threatening illnesses who chose to work with me to live until they died. I asked them to inventory the things that were important to them to do, resolve, and complete before they died. I was using the concept of "unfinished business" as described by Elizabeth Kubler-Ross in her book On Death and Dying and in a workshop I attended with her. Many of my clients' stories were similar to the ones in Kubler-Ross' practice. I learned that people are likely to have 'collected' issues throughout their lives that remain associated with feelings like guilt, resentment, and shame. I was developing a course to teach people how to improve and maintain their mental health. I had this guide in mind as I created that course. Therefore, it was a natural furtherance of my work to include 'clearing away' the barriers of accumulated feelings related to past hurts.

Serious conflicts which are not resolved near when they occur have a way of coming back at various stages of life. Even conflicts that seem relatively minor may take on larger proportions as years go by without forgiveness, acceptance, or some form of closure. Kubler-Ross' early work brought the importance of resolving unfinished business to the attention of health care professionals and chaplains working exclusively with people with terminal illnesses.

Since the time we began to comprehend the importance of resolving old conflicts in our lives, the notion of unfinished business has taken on a broader connotation. Today the term refers to issues that continue to trouble individuals, either consciously or unconsciously, to the extent that lack of resolution interferes with their ability to grow emotionally and/or cope with problems. The energy expended in keeping unfinished business repressed or in continuing to experience the pain it is causing drains the psychological resources you need for healthy adaptation.

Annabel and Mack were a mother and son whose story exemplifies the value of Recognizing and working through unresolved issues. Annabel, a 64 year old physician in private practice, came to my attention when she was diagnosed with a malignancy that was expected to end her life within the year. Annabel's son, Mack, age 28, and the relationship between the two was to become a significant aspect of working with her. Annabel had a lifetime dream that her only child would become a physician and follow in her footsteps. After Mack began accompanying Annabel to some of her sessions and he and I had established rapport, they told me how the strained relationship between him and his mother had developed.

At age 12, Mack had been hospitalized following an accident. While recovering on the orthopedic unit of a hospital, Mack met a male nurse, Richard. The encounter changed both their lives. Until he met Richard, Mack believed all nurses were female. Mack described their first meeting to me something like this:

"Richard walked in, looking like he brought light, confidence, and joy into the room with him. I had been crying and trying to hide it. I was afraid my leg and hip injury would ruin my chance to play football. I couldn't imagine life without football. I pulled the sheet over my head hoping it would dry my tears so he couldn't see them. I wondered what kind of a doctor he was.

> Richard: "I like games. Are you pulling that sheet up to begin a game with me?"
> Mack: (sheet remaining in place) "Do you work with Dr. Duncan?"
> Richard: "You know, as much as I like games, I find it hard to talk with someone without looking at him. Would you mind if we speak face to face?"
> Mack: (pulling sheet down slowly enough to wipe tears if any remained) "O.K. Are you an orthopedist like Dr. Duncan?"
> Richard: "No, I am a Registered Nurse who specializes in working with orthopedic patients."
> Mack: "A NURSE! Geez, I never heard of a male nurse! Are you KIDDING?"

The therapeutic relationship that began that day between Mack and Richard continued through months of painful rehabilitation therapy, the pain of facing that football was over, the anger and frustration of wearing a brace, and the excitement of exploring new possibilities in Mack's future. The leg healed, the brace was discarded, and life resumed a usual pace for Mack even without football. The lessons he learned from Richard about courage, endurance, hope, and how to cope with life remained with Mack far beyond his 12 years. Richard was a 'hero' in Mack's eyes. Mack was determined to be a nurse and have the effect on people's lives that Richard had on his. For a long time, Mack did not tell Annabel.

Mack knew that Annabel was fiercely ambitious for him to become a physician and that his choice to become a nurse would infuriate her. And it did! Mack told her at the end of his Junior year in high school, when he could no longer find ways to deter her constant coaching about how to get into medical school. When a truce was finally reached between them – Mack's final year in his Masters' program in nursing at age 25 – it was due more to his mother's resigned silence than to any true resolution. Mack's father, a physician, had been killed in an auto accident when Mack was 3 years old. Annabel comforted herself by believing that raising Mack without a father was the cause of his "betrayal" of their dream for him. Once Mack's career determination was established, a resigned silence took its place within their relationship like a 'shadow-visitor' - always present, never acknowledged openly.

By the time Annabel told her son about her diagnosis, Richard and Mack were advanced practice nurses working with a thriving new practice association of orthopedists. The two were also becoming close friends. Mack confided his concerns about his mother to Richard, who responded empathetically and said, "Oh, how I hope she forgives you for not being a physician before she dies!" Mack had become so accustomed to the 'silent unspoken' in his relationship with his mother that he had not taken his friend's comment seriously.

Six months later Annabel completed a painful therapy session about her disappointment in her son by writing him the letter I asked her to write. The impact of that letter brought Mack to Annabel's next session, where I met him. Both were angry that I had encouraged her to "dig up this mess!" Annabel virtually yelled at me, "Now look what you've done! My son and I have a funeral to plan, and you've stirred up all this turmoil!"

After the venting, we settled down for some serious work on the unfinished business of Annabel's long-simmering rage at Mack. Two months of probing the unspoken presence in their relationship ensued. Two months in which mother and son learned about one another as adults. As the work went on, Mack began interjecting humor at creative moments, saying things like, "Who are you anyway, Mom? Will the real Annabel please stand up?"

With help, they built their climate of acceptance and used its safety to explore each other's lives in ways neither had dreamed possible. Annabel was at last able to respect Mack's choices about his life, including nursing, and to forgive him for disappointing her. Mack was able to understand that her driving ambition for him had been her effort to show him how much she cared about him and believed in him. He forgave her for her punishing 'silent treatment' response to his career choice. He asked her to forgive him for his passive participation in that treatment.

By the time Annabel became bedridden, she and her son had enjoyed many activities together, learned to be both serious and silly together, and developed a deep respect and abiding confidence in one another. The last time I saw Mack he expressed his gratefulness that he did not lose his mother before he "found out who she was." He shook his head gently, saying, "and all that peace and all that joy may not have been possible if we hadn't faced our big 'nurse' issue. It's amazing, isn't it, how people think something is over just because they quit talking about it?"

You may be surprised I used the word 'forgiveness' to refer to what happened between Annabel and Mack. The word 'forgiveness' may be associated more with your beliefs about spirituality than with your ideas about therapy. As family therapists especially will affirm, forgiveness is a potent concept in working through unfinished business. Years after I worked with Mack and his mother, I found one of the most helpful resources about forgiveness in Dr. Terry Hargrave's book, <u>Families and Forgiveness</u>. Forgiveness for Mack and Annabel was a less complex problem than many we encounter. There are circumstances where issues of forgiveness are more complicated.

For example, there are situations in which one person in a relationship has been deceitful and consciously manipulated the other. The person you feel you need to forgive may have died before you worked out your problems. In some instances, the harm done is considered to be irreparable, as in severe abuse. I find it helpful to distinguish between forgiving the person and forgiving the person's actions. The psychologist Carl Rogers expressed that distinction cogently in his writing about "unconditional positive regard." Acceptance differs from approval, but the two are often so fused in our thinking and in society's way of handling behavior that it takes much effort to tease out the differences.

If a major forgiveness issue is current in your life, I recommend you seek the help of both religious and mental health professionals. The vital point is to recognize the value of bringing issues to some peaceful closure so that you and your elder or other close adult can concentrate on improving your relationship.

There are abundant examples of how family myths and/or family secrets incorporate issues that remain active underneath the facade the family builds to keep them 'smoothed over.' Family myths are stories that present a more acceptable interpretation than the actual happening in a family's history. A family I knew had a myth about an ancestor who was killed in battle. His story as told to succeeding generations was one of heroism in a battle where he was killed. In fact, one of his own soldiers shot him because he was running away (1941 ideas about what constituted treason were simple and concrete). The face-saving version that became the family myth was described to me by that man's great-granddaughter as her 'cross to bear.' She bemoaned her inability to ever do anything brave enough to "live up to the lion-hearted men in our family."

Family secrets may or may not be synonymous with family myths, as the secrets are more likely to be known but not acknowledged by all or most members of the family. Families in which one or both parents suffer from alcoholism are typically filled with such secrets, the primary one being that the parents are unable to control drinking.

Each family has its own difficult issues which often get passed down from one generation to another. Family therapists have written about the uncanny way many of us go out in the world and find a partner whose unfinished family business resonates with our own. The themes that keep resurfacing are often connected with money, sex, violence, alcoholism, desertion, and suicide. In many families, the repeating issue is the source of great pain and misunderstanding.

Significant and traumatic events from our childhood are likely to be among our most vivid memories. Elders sometimes repetitively go over and over such memories as they age. Adults of any age may be preoccupied with childhood traumas. If you are aware of a family issue that you would like to resolve, keep in mind that your childhood memory connected with it is not necessarily correct. It is important to recognize that your feelings about the memory are valid, regardless of the degree of accuracy of your memory of events and behavior. Resolving unfinished business is more often associated with healing the emotions connected with past events than with correcting memory. Catherine and her family, especially her mother, Helen, experienced such a healing of emotions.

Helen was 42 years old when her oldest daughter, Catherine, was approaching her 21st birthday. Helen and her two younger children, Bill (age 10) and Kirsten (age 17) had been working for weeks with William (husband and father) to plan a fabulous "Coming Into Your Own" celebration for Catherine. They wanted it to be a surprise, and a smashing success. Months went into the planning – contacting Catherine's boyfriend and other friends for schedules and ideas for the occasion; lining up grandparents who would attend from out of state; inviting favorite teachers with whom Catherine had been a star pupil; hiring a caterer and a band. As Bill said, "Wow, Mom, it's GREAT when you get to be 21! I can't wait!"

Catherine sensed unusual tension 'in the air.' Musing about what it might mean, she pulled up a childhood memory that periodically recurred over the years. Here is Catherine's memory scene:

Helen and William brought infant Bill home from the hospital. Kirsten jumped up and down with excitement, and she stayed so close it seemed to Catherine she would smother the baby. "I've always wanted a brother – oh, I'm so happy – oh, mama thank you for my brother – oh, I can't wait to hold him," Kirsten went on and on. Catherine had never seen her parents so radiant. When they weren't looking at the baby, they were gazing adoringly at one another. Suddenly, Catherine felt invisible. It was even physical – she felt like no one in the room could have seen her if they had even bothered to look for her. Tears streamed down Catherine's face, but no one noticed. She felt herself shrink back from the happy scene. She retreated to her room when the phone rang and Kirsten grabbed it to be the first one to describe the baby to the grandparent who they were sure was calling. The phone rang frequently all afternoon. Each call was answered with excitement and joyous descriptions of the baby. "Dad, we've finally got a BOY! Our name will go on!"

Catherine heard her father shout through the walls.
Catherine cried herself to sleep that night. No one
noticed that she did not go to the kitchen to eat any
of the array of food friends had brought that morn-
ing. As she sobbed herself to sleep, Catherine felt
utterly abandoned; discarded; alone without a
family.

As the pain of the old memory subsided,
Catherine felt resigned. She thought, "they are
tense because they cannot wait for me to leave.
They are trying to hide how much they want me to
get out – the little happy family of four will be
complete at last! Maybe I won't even wait until time
to move to the dorm; I could get an apartment and
just go ahead and move now. I'd be alone, because
I don't want to live with Jack (boyfriend) but so
what? I've always been the loner in this family.
How much worse could it be?"

Weeks later, when the actual cause of the family tension was revealed and Catherine's huge celebration was over, she wondered why the old, familiar feeling of being alone and abandoned did
not subside. In fact, it became more acute.
Catherine did not yet understand she had so internalized her feelings of rejection and lack of self
worth that objective facts could not penetrate the
labyrinth of her despair.

Many variables went into the development of
Catherine's depression. The day her brother was
brought home and she felt left out was only a part
of them. One specific incident in a life is virtually
never so traumatic that it can account for how that
life evolves. Nonetheless, our lives are made up of
numerous watershed moments. Some result in

'highs,' or peak experiences. Some result in 'lows,' or depressing experiences. On balance, our bio-psychophysiological make up is such that when our whole selves, including our spirituality, is taken into account, we experience an affinity for health. Nonetheless, the ways we deal with our development, coping, and problems may be survival strategies that appear to work for a time yet do not constitute mentally healthy adaptation over time.

Catherine sought help from the counseling center when she enrolled at a local university. She was successfully treated for depression. Working through her unfinished business was one aspect of the therapy she received. It involved learning the difference between her emotions the day Bill was brought home and the feelings about that day recalled by each of her family members. While each family member recalled the day differently, Helen felt guilty about the way Catherine remembered the day.

Catherine's therapist stressed the importance of paying attention to the validity of her own emotions, despite their reminiscences of the same occasion being very different. The family asked Catherine to forgive their insensitivity to her feelings that long-ago day, and she asked them to forgive her harbored resentments of them for her perceived rejection that day. Paying attention to unfinished business can change people's lives and free them up to live their lives from a healthier perspective!

Helen, like many parents, was at first reluctant to delve back into Catherine's memory of the day Bill was brought home. Parents may be reluctant to

discuss matters because they think that acknowl-
edgment of a problem equals blame. Helen was
willing to consider that she had the power to ease
Catherine's mind by facing past difficulties. And it
is rarely too late to do so.

When the therapist treating Catherine for depression requested that Helen and William join
them for a family session, both parents were reluctant to place any value on such an approach. Nonetheless, the healing that took place as they 'heard'
for the first time Catherine's feelings of abandonment and loneliness – despite their perspective
having always been only their love and pride for
her – was profound. They finally understood
Catherine was not blaming them for her feelings,
but needed them to acknowledge that her feelings
were valid. The three cried together and laughed
together as the healing of emotions took place.
The power of unfinished business to affect our lives
is formidable.

Everyone has individual experiences strong
enough to affect the quality of our lives. You are
the one to determine what in your life remains
unresolved, continues to influence your life, and
needs working out. Something that concerns me
enormously in my own life may seem trivial to
others. We need to suspend our individual judgments about what is/is not significant with regard
to unfinished business.

Whatever causes a person to be continually
affected by a 'life moment' that held trauma and
pain needs to come to some sort of resolution that
will help that person let it go – and grow beyond it.
It never occurs to us to wear the same clothes as we

outgrow them. Similarly, we must not expect to fit into the same emotional defenses as we grow. In addition, we will never experience the sheer joy in letting go of outgrown defensive postures until we dare to take our life experiences beyond them.

There are numerous ways to work with unfinished business. I often rely on guided imagery because I find that it is a powerful way to work with unfinished business. Herbert Benson, a physician, has researched relaxation and its results in stress reduction for over twenty years at Harvard. Dr. Benson's research has shown that the body's response to the mind's imagery correlates to its response to actual happenings. When, in the mind's eye, you 'see' yourself in a scenario that recreates an old trauma into a healed response to that trauma, your body, mind, and spirit respond accordingly. It is as if the experience had taken place in the realm of what we call 'reality.'

I do not substitute mental imagery for actual opportunities to work with people in relationship to heal old wounds left by unresolved issues. However, I find that 'practicing' with the use of imagery before an actual confrontation about unresolved issues is extremely valuable. I also find the use of imagery a powerful way to deal with issues in which the other person involved is either dead, or for other reasons inaccessible to the person seeking resolution.

I encourage you to explore methods that can help you deal with unfinished business. As I said, the use of guided imagery is one method I recommend. Another often-used way is to journal about the issue. Describe in your journal as vividly as possible the circumstances surrounding your unre-solved issue. Write all the feelings and memories you associate with the event(s) you described.

Allow yourself time to get in touch with your true feelings regarding the situation, without mak-ing judgments about how you believe you 'should' feel. Meditate on the emotions you describe in relation to your issue until you feel a strong sense of what would help you resolve or release those emotions. Inventory the strengths and resources available to you to obtain what you need. Then make a plan. Structure how you will get the emo-tional closure you need to release – let go of – the issue. Do not hesitate to seek the help of a counse-lor, minister, or trusted friend in Choosing how to carry out your plan.

It is sometimes helpful to describe the differ-ences in how you view your relationships currently versus how you would wish them to be by listing 'now' vs. 'future.' Once you recognize gaps be-tween your real relationship and your ideal of it, ask yourself what it would realistically take to bridge that gap. Then take a serious, practical in-ventory of what it will take to build that bridge. Devise a structured plan to build the bridge, re-membering that you want to build it with healthy behavior. For example, 'peace at any price,' is not healthy. However, negotiated changes on the part of both parties is a mature way to build a bridge between you and others.

There are times when what is needed is a 'real-ity check.' Suppose your unfinished business in-volves a childhood incident, or one that happened long ago. Invite the others who were a part of those moments in your life to recall them with you. I have worked with people who have even found much humor in the differences, once shared, of their perceptions of a specific event. Even if those differences remain, it is possible to come to some understanding that they are significant as evidence of how much our individual perception influences our memories.

One of the most moving stories about unfinished business I have encountered took place when was a consultant at Yale- New Haven Hospital. It was one of the powerful experiences I call 'life moments.' Snippets of time, peak experiences, 'snapshots' lifted from the lives of people I meet create images that move me and remain with me. I collect them, as one might collect precious stones or other articles found in nature. Each one contains lessons within lessons to be gleaned from life – from living. I think of each such encounter as a 'life moment.' Here is a powerful life moment I want to share with you.

Mary, a 73 year old woman with severe heart failure, was a survivor of a 'near death' experience. Admitted to the emergency room (ER) in cardiac arrest, Mary was pronounced clinically dead. Just as Mary's time of death was being called out, a sign of life was noticed on the heart monitor. The ER team responded instantly – and, officially, Mary 'returned from the dead.' Her cardiac problem was so serious it was determined she could not continue to survive without a transplant. The cardiac care unit where Mary was when I met her was an intermediary unit, between cardiac intensive care and a regular medical unit.

In the early 80's when Mary's near-death experience took place, the number of heart transplants was increasing. Ethics committees, transplant teams, and similar groups were developing guidelines for eligibility to receive transplants. A general guideline where Mary was hospitalized was the persons age 70 and over were the lowest priority to receive heart donations. Mary had been on the unit for two days when I was called to see her.

Katherine, Mary's primary nurse, said, "This woman is supposed to be dead. She was brought back to life in the ER. She's nonresponsive. Her vital signs are all right, and we can't tell if her lack of response is because she's more dead than alive or the trauma of what she went through in the ER." Mary was lying on her back with her eyes closed when I entered her room. Her white hair was scattered over the pillow; her gown was awry; her checks were sunken; her color was pale; and her body looked weak and listless. A Bible lay on her bedside table along with a Harlequin novel, a pair of glasses, a tube of lipstick, and a half-eaten cracker. Mary showed no sign of response when I called her name. Something about her remoteness reminded me of catatonic patients I had seen in my early psychiatric nursing days, although her body looked somehow softer.

I pulled up a chair and sat down by Mary's bed. Placing one hand lightly on her wrist, I settled into a relaxed position to become a centered and peaceful presence with Mary. I considered standing and beginning therapeutic touch with her, as I sometimes do with comatose patients. I decided to wait until Mary could respond to me and let me know if I had her permission for that complementary procedure. Sitting by Mary's bed, hoping to make contact with her, I communicated silent thoughts that I wanted to be with her in whatever she was experiencing.

At last, she opened her eyes and looked directly into mine. We maintained eye contact for some time. Our silence and our eye contact felt comfortable. It felt as if we were sharing a moment suspended in time and place. Finally, Mary glanced at my hand on her wrist and asked in a weak voice, "are you from this world or the other one?" "Tell me about the other one," I replied.

"I was dead," Mary stated matter-of-factly. "I heard the people in the ER say I was dead. At first, I didn't feel anything. Then, I felt warm all over and surrounded by a light. It was very peaceful. I just relaxed into it. I wasn't concerned for where I was. I was just THERE! And, wherever that was, it felt good. Then I saw another light like way in front of me – like at the end of a tunnel, like I've read about. I heard a – not a voice – a direction to go toward that light. I went without hesitation – it felt great – it was like floating. I felt happy, peaceful, better than I could ever remember feeling. Just as I got almost to the light, I saw shadows of someone waiting for me behind or on both sides of the light. I got excited. I felt like I was being greeted by people waiting for me to arrive!"

Mary continued, "Before I could move on, I heard someone say, "She's BACK!" I felt terrible pressure on my chest, saw the ER people hovering over me, and thought, "NO — LET ME GO!" I waked up in the Intensive Care Unit. People in green suits were everywhere. Tubes were into my body all over. I was miserable. My chest hurt. I was sorry to be back. I screamed, "Why didn't you let me die?" I heard someone say, "We've got to get a suicide assessment." I thought, "How stupid! Can't they understand that I died, and it was great?"

As I watched this frail-looking woman turn into a little white-haired dynamo as she expressed her emotions about returning to life, I thought about the clarity with which her life energy was now · being expressed. I talked with her about my 'educated hunch' that she had come back because there was something left for her to do or work out. We agreed to work together on the meaning of that near-death experience for her.

At first, she needed to work through her anger at her death being interrupted. "My God, the transplant team sends another dummy in here daily to go over whether I understand how poor my odds are. What are they doing? Practicing talking to near-deathers, I think! It's so inhumane. I was fine with being dead! Can't they at least leave me alone?"

Mary began to tell me her life story. I learned that she was estranged from her only daughter, Jill. An old fight the two had when her daughter divorced her husband of six months had resulted in much trauma for Mary and Jill. Mary had been unable to obtain a satisfactory explanation for the early break up of Jill's marriage, and her anxious efforts to do so exacerbated their fight. So many harsh words were exchanged between the two of them that it had been eleven years since they even tried to communicate. I asked Mary if Jill was aware of the seriousness of her heart condition. "Hell, she's not even aware I'm sick!" Mary replied.

I set up regular times to return for sessions at Mary's bedside. As time went on, Mary and I talked about the meaning of life – and of near-death – to her. She became willing to consider my suggestion that her life may have been saved because there was unfinished business she needed to handle before she died. At last able to say she did not want to die while estranged from her only child, Mary sobbed as she gave me permission to call Jill. Jill was so grateful for word of her mother and for renewed hope for their relationship that she did not even ask me to explain my role with her mother.

In the ensuing weeks after Jill arrived, the three of us spent hours renewing and rebuilding their relationship. One day when I entered Mary's room, her eyes were shining with joy and she looked more 'alive' than I had ever seen her. She said, "You were right. My life was saved so I could have these precious moments with my darling Jill. I've told her about that and also that now I feel like I can die! And that's what I'm telling you. If there is a heart, I want it to go to someone younger than I – and I can die happy now." Mary died the following night. I cried. Jill cried. We hugged in grateful acceptance of life as it is – not perfect, but greatly improved by loving and compassionate connections between people.

Mary's 'life moment' and the brief interval I experienced with Jill remain in my collection of life lessons that encourage me to keep inviting people to share with me the stories in their lives that cry out for reconciliation.

Today's elders are likely to be among a generation that was taught to equate strength of character with ignoring troubles, 'letting bygones be bygones,' and other euphemisms for repression. In
my work with elders, I encounter those who are
scornful of the idea that working on past hurts can
'do any good.' It is important to understand that it
is the painful results being experienced in the
present that we need to work through.

This is not a matter of digging up the past for
no reason. It is a matter of the past intruding on
our ability to live as freely as we might – being as
mentally healthy as we are capable of being. People
are amazingly resilient, and we can and do live and
let go of many of our past hurts and disappoint-
ments. Overcoming adversity is the theme of much
of our most revered drama on stage and in books
and movies. Developing resilience to "the slings
and arrows of outrageous fortune" is a major factor
in a mentally healthy person's life. There is no real
contradiction between being hardy enough not to
'cave in' to life's wounds and being willing to work
toward closure of the ones that remain unhealed.

Steven Levine has written poignantly about
many of his experiences of "meetings at the edge."
I am grateful for my 'meeting at the edge' with
Mary and Jill. It enriched my life. It reinvigorated
my determination to develop a guide for healthy
aging. A little taste of Mary's immortality lives on
now as I relate her story to you.

Although Mary's story is somewhat more dra-
matic than most, there are life lessons in everyone's
stories. Ralph, the professor you met in Chapter 1,
was initially resistant to talking through his grief

about his wife's death largely because he could not believe it would do any good to talk about something he could not change. He was insistent that getting on with life by concentrating on his new marriage was the healthiest thing he could do. "You and your psycho-babble," he said to me. "I can talk 'til I'm blue in the face and it won't bring her back."

Of course talking through his grief did not bring Ralph's first wife back. It did, however, bring his daughter, Angela, back into relationship with him. It helped Ralph and Angela acknowledge and share each other's grief over their loss and feel closer to one another than they ever had. It was influential in building a bridge between Angela and her stepmother, Stephanie. Ralph was able to recognize that he was regaining the energy he had believed he should have as it became less siphoned into the energy it took to repress his true feelings.

There are numerous ways in which resolving unfinished business can enrich our lives. A co-therapist and I once provided marriage and family therapy together in a community setting. We encouraged couples to focus early in the process on agreeing to 'air' their unresolved, often unspoken, conflicts with one another. Sometimes the tension between the two was such that it was best to begin with some structured exercises. For example, writing letters to one another about one unresolved conflict at a time. Their letters were initially shared only in the presence of the therapists. As couples became more skillful and comfortable with effective communication, they became able to negotiate their issues without 'burying' them.

Sometimes I respond to cynicism about the value of working through unfinished business, as I did with Ralph, by asking him to just trust me enough to try it and see for himself. Nor do I assume that elders are the only ones who may be cynical about it. Just try it for yourself – if you find it does not improve your mental health, consider asking a professional to help you with it. Or enlist another pathfinder like myself to help you find your way through the issues.

Be patient with yourself. Use your sense of humor to lighten up about the issues you need to resolve when you can do so authentically. Once you become accustomed to being healthier, you will find that letting go of outworn feelings and nurturing yourself rather than your pain is its own reward!

Chapter 6: Facing the End of the Journey

*"We...must see to it that our deaths become fruitful
in the lives of those who will live after us."*
Henri J.M. Nouwen

In this chapter, we will reemphasize the value of being vitally alive until we die. 'Living until I die' means being mentally and spiritually healthy as long as we live, whatever our physical state. We will discuss practical aspects of preparing for the end of the journey as well as emotional aspects. Vignettes of clients who contracted with me to 'live until I die' exemplify ways to use this approach. This chapter will explore how adults can work through some of their concerns about death in order to create space and energy to enjoy the journey of life.

Journey's ends mark new beginnings: A thought that has comforted me all my life. But this ending? Many of life's endings hold at least 'hints' of what is likely to come next. Completing high school means going to college, or to a job. Weddings mean the beginning of married life. Reaching the ninth month of pregnancy means the approach of a new life. Sending children to college, moving to another state, changing job, even a 'mid-life crisis' – all hold the promise of new beginnings about which we have some idea what to expect.

What we expect about the beginnings ushered in by our physical death is a different matter. Some people say they expect 'nothing.' "That's it; death, and it's just over – everything," one patient told me. For most people, the uncertainty about what they might experience in the process of dying produces far more anxiety than what they believe will happen after they die. The choice we have at the end of the journey is the same as has been throughout – not whether we will do it, but how.

None of us knows when we will die. But unless we have developed an incredible denial system, we have noticed that people eventually die. The older we get, the more we may fear what gerontologists have called the dreadful D's – decline, deterioration, dependency, and death. You may be concerned about what your elders may suffer before they die. Your elder may have said s/he does not want to live "beyond my time," and you are probably aware s/he does not want to suffer. You may be concerned about what your elders may have to endure before they die. In addition, you have the issue of separation to face. Separation or saying good-bye is an emotional issue for both you and your elder. In addition, if you are the elder's child, you struggle with anticipation of life without your parents. You may also feel some guilt associated with the relief that your parent's suffering will be ended by death.

Failure to talk about fears associated with decline, deterioration, dependency, and death tends to increase, rather than decrease, the fears associated with them. Making plans to cope with the "D's" when they occur, can reduce your anxiety and strengthen your ability to cope with changes associated with them. Elders sometimes worry needlessly about limitations they never have to face, thus restricting their ability to engage in activities that bring the most joy into their lives. As an adult who has grown up in a time of extraordinary medical advances, and who probably advocates self care, you might go to the other extreme and over-inflate the possibilities of controlling or delaying death.

People in close relationships who are sharing the journey can help each other talk about the difficult subject of death. I advocate that you and the elder talk about the eventuality of the elder's death in order to:

1. Free up energy that is being used to suppress discussion so that it can be used for living.
2. Help cope with deterioration and other changes if they occur.
3. Ease the process of dying when it occurs.
4. Ease the grieving process when it comes.
5. Pave the way for dealing with unfinished business.
6. Support each other to ease the emotional pain of the experience for both.
7. Seek other support where it is needed.

Your elder is not the only person in your life with whom you are aging. Your fellow travelers on the journey into aging may include your friends, spouse, or partner. Have one or more of them agreed to follow this guide with you through the journey? Another adult who has worked through the territory mapped in the guide and learned to use *RISC* can be especially helpful in preparing you and/or your elder to face the end.

When I began working with clients for the specific purpose of helping them prepare to die, I realized it was my preparation also. As their guide, it was necessary for me to go a little ahead and chart some of the unknown places the journey would take us. It was during those early days of exploring paths to the end of the journey that I first developed *RISC*. Here are some of the things my clients and I learned as we traveled this relatively unknown territory:

- ◆ Denial, our culture's most frequent response to death, is antithetical to experiencing the journey as an adventure all the way.
- ◆ Facing the fact that our bodies will cease to function in this life at some point does not have to be morbid.
- ◆ People vary a great deal in their beliefs about life after death, and what they believe influences how they prepare for death.
- ◆ Making a conscious effort to live until we die sharpens our senses and our awareness of the value of life.
- ◆ We can demonstrate repeatedly the value of the adage, 'live one day at a time.'
- ◆ The sooner we take care of the practical aspects of preparation, the sooner we can relax and increase our enjoyment of living.
- ◆ Conscious living and conscious dying bring our values into sharp focus.
- ◆ Living with integrity is a task that grips us so

completely we do not fall into despair – or, if we do we do not remain there.

♦ As in living our journey into aging, our choice is not whether we will die but rather how we will die.

As you know, there are many beliefs about our after-death experiences. Beliefs range from those who do not believe anything exists after death to those who believe in multiple lives, or reincarnation. Within that broad spectrum, most people have some belief system, religion, or life view that includes some form of survival of our souls after we die. Whatever form those beliefs might take, we do experience the end of our biological existence in the bodies we currently inhabit – we experience death of the present form in which we exist. That occurrence is the point I am calling 'the end of the journey' not because it IS our end, according to my own beliefs, but because it ends our earthly journey as we know it during our current lives.

Death is an experience we can face in a healthy way. Doing so improves the quality of our lives before we die as well as the quality of our deaths.

Hospice workers and others who work with dying and death are familiar with the term, 'a good death.' Yes, a good death is not only possible, but it can be planned for while you are vitally alive and well. In fact, that is the time to plan for it. Morbid? Not at all. This is not about being sad or morbid but about taking a mentally healthy approach to life.

Don't assume that if your elder, or another adult in a special relationship with you, has not brought up the subject of death, that means they don't want to talk about it. You may be aware you have wanted to bring up the subject but failed to do so. Some of the reasons for not bringing up the topic of death that I encounter in working with people are:

+ Fear of worrying or of upsetting the other person
+ Not knowing how to bring it up
+ Being unwilling to expose one's own fears
+ Believing that facing reality means giving up hope and optimism
+ Being taught to be stoic and hide whatever anxiety one has
+ Being unwilling to think about either the other, or oneself, eventually dying
+ Fear that talking about separation and death will bring tears
+ Being unwilling to contemplate life without the other
+ Depending on denial as a major way to cope with unpleasantness in life

Talking about death can be scary. When I taught an undergraduate course in dealing with death and dying, I asked the nursing students to do assignments that helped them get in touch with their own mortality, for example., writing the obituary I mentioned in Chapter 4. It is hard for any of us to help a person who is dying unless we come to terms with our own mortality.

How should you bring up a discussion about death? I have found that one good way to get into the conversation is through a discussion of legal and practical matters.

Practical Matters Associated with Dying and Death

If you have read this far, you have already Recognized that someday you and your loved ones will die. Now it is time to follow that recognition with the next step, Inventory. I recommend you inventory your practical preparation first. By doing your practical preparation now, you will need to revise it over time, but it tends to be easier to revise than to begin. You can tell your elder about what you are doing to initiate a discussion about these matters. It is important that you know about your elder's preparations for death, and you can also use this list to help her or him with that.

As you do your practical inventory, ideas may occur that belong in your broader inventory, such as, "Tell Susan I forgive her." It will be helpful to begin with a list and keep notes on broader and deeper issues that occur as you work through the practical ones. Below is a list of practical matters that should be included. It is not all-inclusive, so add important concerns that occur to you as your make your inventory:

    a. Make a will. If one has been made, check it to ascertain whether it is up to date.

    b. Complete a Durable Power of Attorney for Health Care Decisions. If one has been completed, are there changes in the person or persons you designated to make health care decisions for you in the event you are unable to make them for yourself?

    c. Discuss your wishes thoroughly with the person or persons designated to make decisions in the event you cannot make your own.

d. Complete your Advance Directives, or Health Care Directions, stating what measures you wish to be used to prolong your life in the event your condition prevents your giving such directions yourself.

e. Discuss your Advance Directives in depth with your physician(s), other health care providers, and the person(s) designated in your Durable Power of Attorney for Health Care Decisions.

f. Make a list of items of sentimental value that may not be specified in your will. State the person(s) you wish to receive each item in your list. For example, a rug that is particularly cherished by my granddaughter is to be given to her after I die.

g. List all of your financial assets, e.g., bank accounts, IRA's, or property, and give a copy to one or more of your heirs. Include information about how each asset can be obtained and where the important papers related to it are located.

h. List all charge accounts and their numbers and give a copy to your heir(s).

i. If sentimental papers, e.g., old love letters, are stored in your home place a note on them to instruct the persons who find them how you want them handled, e.g., "Shred these letters when I die," or "Send this journal to Elaine when I die."

j. Write out and discuss with your loved ones any specific directions you want carried out for your funeral. A list of favorite scripture, hymns, poems, and or additional music will be helpful in this matter. State your choice for charitable donations and/or flowers also.

If you are an adult child, you have every reason to encourage your parents to get financial and practical affairs in order and to consult with legal sources when indicated. Discuss with them what they want concerning illness and death, being mindful that their preferences may change over time. You might open the discussion of such matters by saying something like: "There are some things I need to know about how to help you in the future. For example, if you should find yourself so ill that you can't make decisions, who would be your choice to make those decisions for you?" If you have siblings, you may want to add, "Maybe I can help you think this through as to which of us might be most likely to be available to help you."

If you are an elder parent, and you have not discussed end-of-life issues with your adult children, then you need to think very seriously about what is stopping you. You are doing no one a favor, especially yourself, by evading these matters. After serious reflection, you may be aware that you are reluctant to open up old family conflicts and long-time resentments by discussing, for example, who will inherit what when you die.

I assure elders that buried resentments, anxieties, and conflicts will open up anyway when the strain of losing them is bearing upon the family structure. Even if they do not hear issues discussed in their presence, most elders will sense the accompanying tension. Not only that, but the probability conflicts will erupt with bitterness is greater if you have not addressed them calmly before your elder's death is imminent. It is better to grapple with your issues and come to some closure around them so that they can be put aside. Doing so is a part of resolving unfinished business, as discussed in Chapter 5.

By discussing issues like whether or not one wants to be resuscitated in particular circumstances,   an elder can take a step toward relating adult-to-adult with you. However, you may need to be the one to open the topic. By consciously opening up such topics for discussion, you are learning how to cope with the distress of the impending death. At the same time, you are opening the door to more caring and compassion in your relationship. As you free up energy for living by taking care of practical matters, you and your elder will have more energy and freedom to explore adult-to-adult relationships in a variety of healthy ways.

Bear in mind that everything in your preparation for facing the end of the journey is likely to go more smoothly if you carry it out within a climate of acceptance and with the attitude of a person who has chosen_to be a fellow journeyer for your elder or another adult.   The only thing worse than making difficult decisions and putting them behind us is not making them. It helps to remember that all of our decisions will not be perfect. However, by discussing them, you are relating as adult to adult. As you learn how to cope with the distress of impending death by relating to one another in the way this guide leads, you will be opening the door to more caring and compassion in your relationship.

In my private practice, I often asked patients to write a contract with me in which they would pledge to 'live before they died.' The question that followed their agreement was "How do you want to live?" Clients thought of many things they really wanted to do like, see the Smoky Mountains again, or talk to a stepbrother they hadn't seen in 40 years. One woman told me, "I've always wanted to dye my hair blonde."

"Okay," I said, "the next time you come in here I want to see a blonde."
I did.
"Isn't this fun?" she asked, as she entered the room smiling.

Deeper Matters Associated with Dying and Death

You may wonder, "What could be tougher than making a will?" How about something like deciding whether you believe you have made peace with your Creator? Your beliefs may lead you to be more comfortable with contemplating the Divine Force behind the universe; the ultimate One shared by people of all different faiths, or even the agnosticism expressed in 'no belief.' Even if you consider yourself agnostic, you will surely be concerned with how you have lived your life. Perhaps you may wonder nearer the end of the journey whether your lack of belief is 'correct,' or whether you wish to consider exploring faith on a deeper soul level.

Elders often express to me their concern for whether they have fulfilled their purpose in life. In moving accounts of his experiences in a concentration camp, Dr. Victor Frankl wrote about differences he observed in those who survived, as he did, and those who died. He was so struck by the importance of finding meaning in suffering and in life that he founded a school of psychotherapy based on "man's search for meaning." (Frankl, 1964).

I recommend you, your elder, and other adults who choose to share your journey have periodic discussions about what I call 'the deeper issues.' Doing so need not be depressing, too 'heavy,' or any of the usual negative descriptions people use to avoid such discussions. Here are some guidelines about approaching these deeper issues with your fellow traveler:

- ◆ Trust is absolutely essential. Your discussions will involve your most deeply-held thoughts, beliefs, and feelings. You and the adult with whom you discuss them must trust one another to value their meaning to you and to respect differences in your approaches to living/dying.
- ◆ Agree on the amount of time you will spend – not rigidly adhering to a schedule, but providing a safe 'space' in which both of you know approximately how long each discussion will last. Intense topics are, like seasoning, best approached in small amounts that add 'spice' to life. You can have as many discussions as you choose over time. Reaching a 'stopping point' in a deep discussion without being exhausted will add to your enjoyment of looking forward to the next one.
- ◆ Agree on the environment in which such discussions will take place. Choose favorite spots, for example, in the woods, on the beach, in a restaurant, or a separate room at home where you feel relaxed and peaceful. Depending on individual preferences, some people favor returning to the same place for all such discussions while others prefer to

vary their environments. Keep in mind that your discussion is the focus. This is not a 'tourist moment.'

♦ Bring each deep discussion to closure by mentioning topics you plan to ponder in the times between such discussions. Doing so will add richness to your exchanges as well as help you recognize concerns you want to bring to such moments.

♦ Inject humor when it feels natural. For example, a good laugh about what could be on your tombstone (if you plan to have one) vs. what probably will actually be on it can lighten things up in a healthy manner.

♦ Seek advice, counsel, and therapy when appropriate. Issues that arise in these discussions may be sensitive and/or complex enough for you to seek a professional to discuss them. For example, it may be wise to seek a minister, rabbi, or similar religious professional to help you with theological, moral, and philosophical concerns related to faith. Seeking the assistance of a therapist may also be wise if either of you are dealing with psychological conflicts which have roots in your earlier life or if you are in serious emotional turmoil. Legal advice may be needed for complex financial situations or decisions regarding custody care for a spouse with dementia. Your close relationships will be important sources of support for you if you are receiving professional assistance. If, instead of seeking professional help for yourself, you are urging your elder to do so, s/he may need a lot of encouragement because of the bias against therapy mentioned in an earlier chapter.

♦ Provide for emotional 'cooling off' periods. No matter how well you and your elder or another fellow traveler may be, neither of you will profit from attempting discussions in the 'heat of battle.' If you find yourselves fighting, declare a truce. Return to the section on dealing with anger in Chapter 4 and follow the tips in the guide related to managing anger. Follow up your anger management by making arrangements for continuing your in-depth discussions about your lives.

♦ Keep in mind that your deep discussions are for the purpose of helping you and your fellow travelers share the journey into aging and face the end of the journey. The deep discussions can assist you to do what Steven Levine calls "conscious living and conscious dying." They are not mountain-top experiences where you expect to receive 'answers' about the universe from an all-knowing guru.

As each of you explore your life, make an inventory of the regrets you uncover, the new areas you want to discover, and anything that arises regarding the quality of your life. My clients made a realistic 'wish list' as part of their Inventory. It was sometimes as frivolous as the woman who wanted blonde hair and often much more serious. I asked them to complete the statement "Before I die I want to _____."

This is a good time for you to stop reading and begin a page in your journal by writing "Before I die I want to _____." Fill in the blank with the first things that come to mind, as you will add to the list later. If you are not keeping a journal, begin a blank sheet of paper with the statement and keep it as you continue to read. It takes a full lifetime to finish the Inventory, so do not consider it a finished document at any time.

Elizabeth Kubler-Ross's work with dying people is well known, and she has held numerous seminars on facing death and working with the dying. She delineated five stages that she observed in her dying patients: 1) Denial and Isolation 2) Anger 3) Bargaining 4) Depression and 5) Acceptance. It is important to know that experiencing any emotions in any stages is normal. People cycle through the stages and must not be expected to 'march' through them in an orderly fashion. The stages are not linear. Many variables influence the ways in which people experience each stage, and we often return to the same ones again and again.

Dianne was a person who I helped to manage her rage about a cancer diagnosis and mastectomy. Dianne was a 36 year-old accountant with a large banking firm in New York City.   She had postponed her marriage to Tony, one of the bank's Vice Presidents, three times since age 29. Immersing herself in her career in order to get promotions were Dianne's reasons for the first two times she asked Tony to postpone their wedding. The third occasion was due to the surgery that she was told would remove a small "pre-cancerous growth" in her breast.

When I asked Dianne to Inventory the things about which she was angry, she yelled, "Damn it! If I had that much control, I wouldn't be this upset, would I?" I suggested she just start yelling them out, and I would write the Inventory as she did so. By the time she got to the end of her list, she had expended enough energy to speak somewhat more calmly about it.

In the ensuing two weeks, we did in-depth work as she recuperated from the surgery. Tony joined us for hour-long sessions scheduled to coincide with his visits. He summed up his impressions by saying: "I think we've got it licked now. Dianne needed to get all that poison out of her system. Now we can get on with our lives. I want to concentrate on planning our wedding now. I think I've convinced her I love her, and not just her breast, don't you?"

Nice try, Tony. Unfortunately, life is not so simple. Tony read Kubler-Ross's book, <u>On Death and Dying</u>. He concluded, as others have, that his fiancee would make an orderly progression through the next two stages and arrive at 'Acceptance' in time for a Spring wedding. It was a challenge to help Tony understand that he could not run his life like he ran his bank. He agreed to come to my office weekly for short-term therapy while Dianne was recuperating at the home of an aunt who lived nearby.

On his second visit, Tony stated the session would be his last. Obviously frustrated, he stated flatly, "This talking stuff simply does not work!" Probing a little, I learned that he had returned to find Dianne even more angry than when she 'got over it' in the hospital. There is much more to Dianne and Tony's story. The point I want to make here is that the added stress of recovery from her mastectomy, the need to work through her grief about losing her breast, her anxiety about what would happen to her life, and planning a wedding were more than Dianne could handle. Her recurring anger 'stage' was a signal that she needed in-depth strategies to help her cope.

Several months later, Dianne was in therapy with someone to whom I referred her in New York City. She and Tony were attending a support group for cancer survivors. During the next three months she kept me informed about her progress. Dianne cycled back and forth between anger, bargaining, acceptance, and depression many times. In her last telephone conversation with me, she laughed a little and said, "Well, at least, I didn't spend much time in denial; so I guess I'm doing pretty well with it after all." Dianne and Tony both 'did well' as they learned to understand the meaning of what they were going through and to use the concept of the Kubler-Ross stages to inform, and not to judge, their life experiences.

Exploring for oneself and with one's loved ones such deep topics as the meaning of suffering, the meaning of illness, and the meaning of life involves virtually endless possibilities. The sooner we begin exploring the journey by delving into some of our deeper issues, the better. Energy drained by "if only I had..." is energy we can put to better use by beginning right now to live fully.

Sharing at Journey's End

Let's take a look at a couple who began sharing the journey's end by completing the statement, "Before I die, I want to ____." Lionel, Sr. and his wife, Beth, were a couple in their 70's who chose to complete the statement together. Lionel was hospitalized and considered in end-stage renal failure when I met them. Their first line read: "Before I die, I want us to be at peace about our son, Lionel, Jr., and to see him again to forgive him for being gay."

Lionel and Beth Harrison were strong Southern Baptists who believed themselves 'liberal' because they had four African-American neighbors, one of whom belonged to their church. They lived in a suburb of Houston, where Lionel had been a mechanic and Beth taught second grade until they retired. They had three other children, Alice, Evelyn, and Bill, who were ages 51, 48, and 46 respectively. They regretted not naming Bill after his father until six years later, when Lionel, Jr. was born.

The couple discovered Lionel, Jr., was homosexual when he brought his boyfriend home from college during his Freshman year at the University of Texas. Shock is too mild a word to describe their reactions. The words they used were: "ashamed, embarrassed, outraged, and betrayed." They strongly believed homosexuality was a sinful choice their son had made and that, in making it, he had betrayed them and his Christian upbringing. Lionel, Sr. ordered his son and his partner to leave at once, shouting, "I disown you! You have disgraced me, and I never want to see you again," as they exited.

Years later, as Lionel faced the end of his journey with his failing kidneys and options expended, the topic of disowning their son remained a source of contention between Lionel and Beth. "I know Lionel, Jr. is wrong; but I can't forgive his daddy for kicking him out of the family," Beth told me. "And," she added, "I don't want Lionel to die with me mad at him."

As you see, Lionel and Beth and their family had a story poignantly filled with deeper issues. Their Inventory included the following strengths and resources:

a. A long and essentially stable marriage and love for one another
b. Three older children whose beliefs about Lionel, Jr. had not been explored
c. Lionel, Jr. had continued to write brief notes to his parents just to say he loved them
d. Lionel, Jr. was in a stable relationship that had lasted several years
e. Bill stated he wanted to get to know and understand his brother, Lionel, Jr.
f. A mental health counselor was available who worked exclusively with gay couples
g. A protestant minister was available who had education and experience in family counseling. Although the minister was not Baptist, the Harrison's minister said he could "tolerate" their going to him for counseling
h. The medical estimate of Lionel, Sr.'s life span was at least another month to six weeks
i. All members of the family believed strongly in forgiveness

Lionel, Sr. was discharged from the hospital and sent 'home to die.' At his bedside, all the family except Lionel, Jr. met with me and the minister who did family counseling. We discussed the Inventory the parents had completed in the hospital.

We went to the next step, **Structuring**. We made a plan that included contacting Lionel, Jr. about his father's condition, how the family would learn about homosexuality from the mental health counselor, and how Lionel, Jr. would be brought back into the family structure if he were willing. We delayed the decision about whether Lionel, Jr.'s partner would be considered a family member until after they worked with the mental health counselor.

We spent three weeks on the beginning of the structure. Lionel, Jr. responded promptly with a note that said he was grateful for the information and, as his notes always had, said he loved his parents. We all said a prayer of thanksgiving together that love was, despite all the pain, proving to be the strongest family value.

During our fourth week, Lionel, Jr. and his partner were invited to join the family for a meal and some healing conversation centered on loving and forgiving even if understanding did not become possible. In the ensuing two weeks, the family gathered every day or two at Lionel's bedside. They played old home movies, read favorite scriptures and other books aloud, played Charade, ate Beth's "family soothing food," as she called it, and shared information about what was happening in each of their own lives and families. They watched comedies on television and laughed together at the antics of Lucy and others. Sometimes they cried, sometimes they argued, sometimes they all sat silent, sometimes they laughed – in other words, they lived, as did Lionel, Sr., until his death.

I do not know what happened in the Harrison family after Lionel, Sr died. I do know that, before he died, I saw him laugh, hug all his children, tell his wife he was at peace with her and thank her for a long and good marriage, and say, "I forgive you, son, and I love you," to Lionel, Jr. "A good death," our hospice colleagues might say.

If all the children had not lived in the area, our structure would have been different. Nonetheless, the ingredients could have remained the same. Email exchanges might have replaced some of the gatherings, old family photo exchanges might have been necessary by mail or computer; and not all the emotions could have been exchanged together in the group. The clear choice the Harrison family made was to spend their remaining time together reconciling their differences and being a healthy family.

And, yes, it must be said – one or more of them could have found they could not bring themselves to forgive. Remember, our behavior is the only behavior we can control. Vignettes from people's life stories cannot tell it all. Nonetheless, from over twenty years of experience, I have hundreds of excerpts from the lives of real people who took the *RISC*. They, as well as I, have been grateful they showed the courage and endurance to risk being vitally alive.

One of the most valuable lessons I have learned working with dying and death concerns the help-lessness people feel surrounding death. Much of the discomfort loved ones feel when someone close to them is dying is associated with feeling that they have become 'helpless' to do anything for that person – that they can no longer be 'of any use.' Physicians, nurses, and other health care givers often share the feeling even though they can oc-cupy themselves with palliative measures that allay the vulnerability of 'helplessness' to some extent.

The enormous feeling of vulnerability of dying is shared by all who 'stand by,' helpless to stop the process.

The value of energy shared by sheer presence cannot be overemphasized. Your very presence with your loved one during dying and death is a supreme gift in itself. When I participated in a workshop with Steven Levine on "Conscious Living and Conscious Dying" this valuable lesson was reinforced. For example, Steven taught us how to use synchronized breathing with the dying person to communicate our presence with them more explicitly.

A nurse, Sarah, on the neurological unit at Yale-New Haven Hospital called me about the distress she noted in the wife of a man who was in a coma and not expected to survive. Sarah told me "Mrs. Yarborough and her husband have been married for 45 years. They have no children, and their lives have been very much bound up with one another. Doug has an inoperable brain tumor. He has been unresponsive for 72 hours, and his wife, Nancy, gets more anxious by the minute. She refused the medication Doug's physician offered her for anxiety, but she cries, stares at him, follows us around, and begs for 'something to do' almost constantly. I don't know whether her husband is aware of her anxiety, but it's driving the staff 'crazy.' What can you do?"

I invited Nancy to leave the unit to join me for coffee and tell me about herself and her husband. Nancy spoke and breathed rapidly as she enumerated the many activities and interests she and Doug had shared for so many years, ending each recitation with, "... now it's over. We'll never do that again. What can I do?" She accepted my suggestion that we go to my office and work on calming down her breathing. Nancy was accustomed to following her husband's lead in activities. That habit worked in our favor as she did exactly what I directed her to do. I taught her a basic relaxation exercise that showed her how she could invoke her own body's relaxation response, as described by Dr. Herbert Benson.

Nancy agreed to sit at her husband's bedside and practice her relaxation response at least once each hour. By the time I arrived at his bedside the following day, Nancy reported some improvement in her feelings. However, she still felt distraught because she could "do nothing" for Doug. I taught her to stand by his side and watch his breathing, synchronizing her own with his. She discovered, as people usually do, that an incredible feeling of energy exchange and closeness can take place when doing synchronized breathing. Nancy expressed amazement at "how close I feel to him."

If you have a situation in which you decide to try synchronizing your breathing, you will learn it is not as easy to do as it looks to someone observing you. I recommend practicing with your loved one just to get the feel of it long before you need to use it in the dying process. If you practice at home, your loved one will be able to lie down on a lower bed, so that you can sit when you practice. Your chest needs to be at about the same level of the other persons, and if they are in a hospital bed this usually means standing by their side. If you are too shy to practice beforehand, you can still use it when you and your loved one need it most.

Often, people are conscious right up until moments before they die. How do you talk about the end of the journey? Beren was a client who contracted with me to 'live until she died.' She often talked with me about dreading her "last few hours" with her family. Her husband, Ted; her son, age 19; and two adopted daughters, ages 13 and 15, described themselves as a close family who had joyful times together when Beren's cancer was in remission. Overall, the Martin family successfully lived their lives even though they were periodically interrupted by frightening episodes related to Beren's cancer. Nonetheless, she continued to experience dreading those last few hours which were expected to come within the year.

I suggested Beren write a letter to each of her loved ones when she felt well and save the letters to be given to them either in her last hours or after her death. Never one to shy away from challenges, Beren took that suggestion very seriously. She worked on her letters for two months, smilingly referring to them as "my labor of love – harder than childbirth." She returned often after thinking a letter was completed to add something important. Beren expressed her gratefulness at living long enough to write the letters, adding "even if I'd tried, I never could have remembered to tell them all these important things at the very end."

As her condition deteriorated, I asked Beren to think with me about her hopes for the exact cir-cumstances at the moment of her death. "What a relief to be asked that question," Beren replied. "If I can have my hopes, I want the children to come in, receive their letters from either me or Ted. I want each one to kiss and hug me and say out loud, "good-bye," and anything else they want to say. My letters will speak for me. Then I want them to go to a room nearby and read their letters and stay there together until their father comes to tell them I'm gone. I want to die holding Ted's hand with one, yours with the other, and with Father James praying aloud." And that is exactly how it happened.

Everyone does not have the opportunity (or even the capability) to face the end of the journey with as much clarity as Beren and her family did. Nor does everyone have the circumstances work out as precisely as they did in the Martins' case. Nonetheless, in my experience I see that facing the end with as much clarity as possible is more likely to assist all people involved. It is more likely to help the dying person have a 'good death.'

It is helpful to keep in mind that our Western culture encourages denial of death. Increasingly, businesses and other influences develop sanitized approaches and euphemisms to replace older rituals of dealing with death. Some other cultures seem to have held more closely to their rituals of hundreds, or thousands, of years. As we hear more and more about our shrinking planet, it is worth contemplating that we may be losing these long-treasured rituals globally. If so, we would do well to redevelop rituals suited to the current times, because rituals help the dying and their survivors cope with the end of the journey.

Your religious preferences will, of course, affect your choice of rituals. This is not about which is 'right' vs. 'wrong.' It is about paying attention to the importance of ending the journey with rituals that are valued by the loved one who is dying. As a survivor, you will be able to find comfort in participating in your loved one's final ritual(s) simply by your compassionate understanding of its importance to your loved one.

You may be a person who fears discussing death because you might cry when you talk about it. Ask yourself: "What emotion is appropriate to losing someone I love?" Sadness, grief, and sorrow are terms that will likely come to your mind. Tears are appropriate to those feelings and are an outlet for them that is provided by your body's physical nature.

As a professional, I was taught that I must never show my emotions when dealing with a patient. Following the death of one of my first patients, I was scolded by my supervisor: "You make up your mind! You cannot be a nurse and be the mourner too!" My internal guide responded, "Why not?" Pondering that incident over the years, it seems to me that failing to respond with sadness when a life is lost is a strange notion of how we value human life.

Our tearful response is an expression of our caring and compassion. And take it from me – it is entirely possible to cry and work at the same time. In addition, if you cry, you may give permission to your loved one to allow her or his tears to flow too. Tears wash the soul and clear our eyes to see clearly and compassionately what we need to see about life. And that is our goal – to live, and to be fully alive.

When someone is dying, people sometimes tell me "I just don't know what to say." There are no prescriptions here. The nature of the relationship you have with the dying person is probably your best indicator of 'what to say.' In a close relationship and when you have shared your journey into aging, you have learned what it is comfortable to say to each other. I recommend avoiding ghoulish humor, lying, and outright denial of reality. Your shared relationship has not been phony if you and your elder have shared the journey and followed this guide. Authenticity has been a hallmark of your relationship throughout the journey. It will provide all the guidance you need for 'what to say.'

On the other hand, you may find yourself saying 'good-bye' to someone with whom you had a poor relationship. If that is your situation, you may be able to express genuine regret by saying something like "I'm sorry we didn't get along better, and I hope we can forgive one another for any pain in our relationship." If the failure to have had a better relationship blocks your expressing yourself when the death is near, I suggest you seek help from a chaplain or other spiritual counselor or therapist.

Of course, it is not true that all endings can be upbeat, but do your best. Whatever the nature of your relationship, I encourage you to seek help with your grieving. It is often wise to attend a bereavement group, seek grief counseling, and/or work through unresolved grief issues with a counselor or therapist.

In general, we need to tell our loved ones as much as we can about what sharing the journey with them has meant to us. We need to thank them for the value their relationship has added to our lives. We need to work out any unfinished business by using ideas such as those in Chapter 5 of this guide. We need to have light, peaceful moments with them if possible.

Trust your relationship; remain true to yourself and to your loved one; and the words will come. If they will not come out aloud, write them. Draw, or find pictures that express them, find cards that express them, give little gifts that express them, be creative. Your loved one will get your message. That is another reason why the climate of acceptance you two created earlier is so important.

Depending on your beliefs, you may find it comforting and authentic to speak to your dying loved one about a life hereafter. When my friend, Betty, was dying, we said to one another, "See you on the other side." That was comforting because we both believe in eternal life. If you are not comfortable with perceiving things that way, just be real.

A woman I knew was still working toward forgiving her husband when she died. At the end, she told him, "God and I are going to keep working on it 'til we get it right." A daughter I knew said to her mother at the end "Thank you for bringing me into the world, Ma. I really like living." The radiance of her smile, through her tears, said it all.

Epilogue: A Fable

I am Helena – a turtle. I want very much to be an unusual turtle; but I suppose I am quite ordinary. My legs are too short; my head is sort of 'sunk in' to my shell. My shell makes me look stronger than I am. I get tired sometimes of feeling it weigh me down. Turtles are said to be slow but also durable. There's a story about a tortoise winning a race with a hare by being patient and steady – durable.

In my dreams, my shell is light as a feather. I can run and jump, holding my head high. There are myths about turtles that could fly; turtles used by wise men to foretell fates – stories like that. Turtles in myths do things real turtles cannot do. Myths are like that. Still, myths contain ancient truths about the nature of the world that wise people ponder.

Other turtles tell me, "You are a nice turtle. Be satisfied with who you are. Why should you want to fly? Turtles are not supposed to fly! What difference does it make?" What difference? The difference between being like all other turtles and being who I am. I can try to fly and be as much as I can like what I know inside myself. I will begin by giving myself an identity – a name. I will no longer

simply call myself a turtle. I will be called Helena! I
like that name – it reminds me of stories about
Helen of Troy. I am Helena!

In some cultures, turtles are symbols of patience. Turtles are symbols of longevity. Those are
properties of turtles much to be desired. What can
I become if I reframe my notion of myself: a symbol
of patience; or a seer; or a turtle whose flights of
fancy are so vivid they add a quality of 'specialness'
to life. I belong to a species of turtles that are long-
lived. I have time: time to wait for death to come –
OR – time to find meaning in living – to search for
the truth in the ancient stories passed along
through the wisdom of the ages.

*Children exploring a remote beach came upon
an ancient turtle and mourned its death as children
do. They asked relatives about the turtle they had
found. They were told she had been called "Helena"
for reasons no one remembered. The villagers gathered to mourn Helena, and to tell stories about her.
They had learned the stories from their grandparents – who knew how much was truth, how much
myth?*

*Helena was said to have moved faster and held
her head higher than anyone had ever seen a turtle
do. Parents taught their children about Helena as an
example of patience. Turtles were plentiful on the
beach, especially when laying their eggs, but Helena
was called 'special.' Children sometimes declared
they had seen her smile, watching carefully as children do. Whatever it was that was special about her
was a mystery.*

An old man in the village said it was true that Helena was very special, very old, and would be very missed now she was dead. He said she must be buried with a special marker placed on her grave. The village gathered for a ceremony to pay homage to Helena. A marker was found for her grave. "What should it say?" the village chieftain asked the wise old man. "It should say 'Helena was an unusual turtle. She taught us many things by her living. She will be missed.'"

Appendix for Mental Health Professionals

Purpose

The purpose of this Appendix is to address issues frequently encountered in the use of the model. It is not intended to be professional direction to your practice as an independent mental health professional. Standards of practice in your specific mental health discipline will be your frame of reference for supervision. This Appendix is written for persons who have completed formal educational and supervised training experiences in the fields of Advanced Psychiatric-Mental Health Nursing, Clinical Psychology, Psychiatric Social Work, Marriage and Family Therapy, and Psychiatry. No instruction in your particular mental health discipline would be professionally appropriate here, and none is implied or intended by the author.

If you have chosen to participate in the workshop and/or to read the book to discover how the model works for you in your own clinical practice, then you have self-selected as an individual practitioner. You are, therefore, capable of collaborating with your professional colleagues in a manner congruent with your discipline. You are also likely to be a mental health professional who is open to innovative ways to help your clients. I hope you will share with me your experience using the model. This work will be enriched by exchanges among those of us who use it from our different perspectives within the climate of acceptance described in the model. My contact information is on the last page of this Appendix.

The Model

This book presents, in lay-person's terms, the basic concepts underlying a didactic model. The work is an interactive growth model that has been forged from two decades of advanced clinical practice with elders and their children, spouses, and close friends. My clients were encountered in the community, in private practice, and in hospitals and clinics. The conceptual framework was devised as a specific clinical intervention to be taught to and by mental health professionals for use with their elderly clients and families. Initially conceived as a parent/child intervention, the model evolved with far broader application to become a model for healthy aging. The initial material was developed to be used only in a workshop format, with mental health professionals facilitating the workshops. Feedback from mental health professionals and my own clients spurred its growth into the current, multifaceted form presented in this book.

Adult children, predominately of the 'boomer' generation, many of whom were also professionals, grasped the application of the model to their own aging and spurred the expansion of the initial work. Their vision grasped the value of a guide for healthy aging which their generation can immediately apply. The potential for implementing proactive health measures and building a mentally healthy life became the exciting outgrowth of "Aging as a Shared Journey" in its present configuration.

The qualitative data used to develop the model were extrapolated from my clinical practice data. Outcomes were recorded in anecdotal form as reported by elders and their families who were learning how to apply the *RISC* strategy to deal with the various elements of the model listed below. Case vignettes were developed to illustrate various applications of the model to health assessment, psychotherapy, therapeutic alliance with families, and teaching and counseling parents and their adult children, spouses, and friends.

Although this interactive, experiential work is dynamic and evolving, "Aging as a Shared Journey" is solidly grounded in a conceptual framework founded on lifespan development theory and strongly influenced by interpersonal relationship theory. The popular phrase, 'becoming your parents' parent' is not only antithetical to the model but potentially damaging to the health of all adults. The misguided notion extends existing stereotypes and facilitates behaviors that are not in the best interest of anyone's mental health.

Basic Premise of the Model

1. Aging and changing the balance of dependence/independence require new approaches to relating to one another as adults.
2. Both adults in a relationship are aging: you and your client; you and your parents; and you and your spouse, friend, partner, or any

other adult with whom you are connected closely.

3. At any age, a parent is still a parent. The roles you and your parent take may change over time, but reversing the roles denigrates the value of your parent/child bond.

4. Changes in functional status that may occur in association with illness and/or disability as people age are not synonymous with similarities in emotional, psychological, or spiritual development. For example, an adult with weakened sphincter control who wears protective undergarments is still an adult – not an infant in 'diapers.'

The terminology of building a conceptual model has been adapted to lay terms throughout the book. For example, the components, or elements, derived from the theoretical framework are described as different territories, or areas of the terrain of aging being explored. The phenomena of aging, the biopsychosociophysiologic processes as well as the spiritual/emotional components, are conceptualized as a journey. The model for healthy aging becomes, in lay terms, the guide for healthy aging. The adult who chooses to experience aging as a healthy journey, shared with significant others, becomes the pioneer who is helping explore the territory of aging. The didactic terminology is retained in the Appendix, which is addressed to you as a professional.

Conceptual Framework of the Model

The therapeutic context within which the work inherent in the model is to be done involves two foundational concepts for both you and your clients:

a) heartwork and b) building and maintaining a climate of acceptance. You will be more accustomed to thinking of these concepts as the rapport, reflection, introspection and insight that are facilitated by a therapeutic alliance with your clients.

As mentioned in the Introduction and Overview, Erik Erikson and his associates developed a theoretical framework of life cycle development based on eight stages through which each of us progresses from birth to death. The last – which involves resolving the tension inherent in Ego Integrity vs. Despair – challenges the individual to rework the tensions and rebalance the strength of all earlier stages. By doing the reworking and rebalancing, the individual attempts to "establish an integrity of the self" that both draws sustenance from the past and remains vitally involved in the present.

Mid-life adults, the target audience for this book, are in a more powerful phase of life. Erikson described their developmental task, Generativity vs. Stagnation, as 'taking care of' institutions, professions, and families. He and his associates emphasized that the world is in the hands of mid-life adults. They belong to the generation that most 'caregiver burden' literature addresses. Being in different stages, confronted with different life tasks can create a gulf between generations. The choice to collaborate as fellow travelers in intergenerational pursuits is a healthier approach. I find that adults of all generations are able to support one another as they release outmoded roles and establish a sense of connection by applying this adult - adult model.

Hildegard Peplau's theory of Interpersonal Relationships extended the work of Harry Stack Sullivan and demonstrated the power of establishing a therapeutic alliance with patients. The professional nurse's role with psychiatric patients was initially grounded in Peplau's theory. As an interdisciplinary team approach to psychiatric treatment developed, professionals outside nursing, e.g., psychiatric social workers, began to include Peplau's theory regarding the use of the therapeutic relationship. Peplau's work lends itself to extending the concepts related to development of a therapeutic alliance and promoting healthier relationships in families and other adult associations. Such concepts are integrated into teaching how to use the model to share the journey.

The work of Mary Baird Carlsen served as a paradigm for me in developing a clinical model based on clinical practice experience. Her brilliant melding of theory and practice and her use of developmental and constructivist theories provided me with direction in building my conceptual framework. In addition, her comprehension of the value of meaning-making to elders confirmed my own clinical findings substantially.

As a professional, you will recognize the integration of Erikson, Peplau, Carl Rogers and other theorists into the elements of the model. My qualitative data base began with 65 parent/child dyads. As my practice continued, data were derived from other adult-to-adult clients, e.g., spouses, friends, and partners. The total number of relationships included in my data base was approximately 150. Data were subjected to content analysis, from which recurrent themes were derived. The dominant themes that emerged from the analysis became the elements of the model.

The Model as Clinical Intervention

Sequential Use of the Model

The order in which the elements are addressed depends on variables in each unique relationship. Ideally, participants are introduced to the model in the workshop format of two full days. During the workshop, they receive guidelines about how to work through the elements in the sequence they are presented in the book as well as how to put a higher priority on a particular element for their ongoing journey into aging. For example, adults who are related as parent/child, spouses, partners, or intimate friends may begin the work knowing that one of them has a life-threatening illness. In those cases, you will recognize the importance of putting a high priority on the elements "Resolving Unfinished Business" and "Facing the End of the Journey."

When you are working with clients known to you through your practice, your knowledge of the history of the clients and your assessment of their mental health needs will determine the sequence in which you address each element with them. At the very beginning it is imperative to establish the climate of acceptance and to teach the clients how to use *RISC*. Regardless of the sequence you use, I implore you to keep in mind that the elements are interwoven. Working with any one of the elements will bring up concerns related to the others. The element of "Communicating Clearly and Compassionately" is a thread that runs throughout each segment of the work. Approach each element from the perspective that the elements are always interrelated.

Emphasize that **RISC** will be used throughout, because each element will bring up new ways in which it can be applied. Your therapeutic relationship with your clients should demonstrate the importance of the climate of acceptance. Follow up your initial rapport by being intentional in discussing how you and your clients will build and maintain a climate of acceptance.

Having taught your clients how to use **RISC,** you will be guided by your knowledge and assessment of the clients regarding which element should be a beginning point. Unless your assessment indicates an urgent reason to begin with one specific element, for example, "Resolving Unfinished Business", it is advisable to begin working through the elements sequentially, as they are ordered in the book.

Assessment

Your particular mental health discipline will influence your choice of assessment tools. Your reliance on such tools as a battery of psychological tests, the Diagnostic and Statistical Manual (DSM), and/or assessments such as the Beck Depression Inventory (BDI) will depend on your professional education and experience. Using the tools and methods that you value and those you find most helpful when determining a treatment plan for your clients, your assessment should include but not be limited to the following:

1. Cognitive Function: Determine that your clients' cognitive function is intact to the extent necessary to using this education approach. Effective results with this model depend on the ability to: a) learn communication skills, b) practice stress management, c) make and follow through on plans for changing behavior, and d) understand the concepts inherent in the model. Determine how your clients' cognitive status is likely to have an impact on their ability to:

    a. learn *RISC* and use it appropriately

    b. use feedback, i.e., verbal responses and cues from you and others and/or videotaping, to improve communication skills

    c. learn strategies, e.g., cognitive restructuring

    d. set goals (with your guidance) for trying out new behaviors and changes

    e. learn relaxation exercises and related stress management techniques

    f. make application of what can be learned through the case vignettes

Note: Keep in mind that "Aging as a Shared Journey" is essentially a mental health model. It has not been used as presented in this book with any persons whose cognitive status was significantly impaired.

2. Behavioral/Emotional Function: Determine that your clients have sufficient ego strength to manage an approach that involves self-examination, with your support. Develop an individualized plan for managing anxiety, anger, or other potential emotional sequelae of implementation. Your clients

should be able to respond favorably to therapy that
involves:

    a. taking responsibility for personal behaviors
    b. recognizing and respecting differences with
        other adults in relationships
    c. increasing self esteem
    d. reporting results of using the strategies in
        order to assist in ongoing evaluation

3. Psychiatric Status: The persons in the
sample used to develop this model were medical
and surgical patients and clients from the community. Actively psychotic individuals were excluded
from the sample. With clients who have a psychiatric diagnosis, determine their ability to use this
model by their functional status. Use your clinical
judgment to determine whether a client's psychiatric illness contraindicates the use of this model. I
found the use of the model highly effective with
clinically depressed clients, many of whom were on
a combined treatment plan of medications and
cognitive brief psychotherapy. Individuals who had
been treated for psychiatric illnesses in the past,
e.g., bipolar illness, responded favorably when they
developed trust in the therapist and in the process.
Persons who carried such diagnoses as "borderline
personality disorder" helped me identify the flaws
in the model through their efforts to manipulate
both the therapist and the process.

4. Baseline Data: Prior to introducing your
clients to the model, check to ascertain that you
have a minimum of the following information
about each client:

    a. Biographical information that includes, if
        possible, history of family of origin
    b. Cultural background, especially if client is a

member of a minority culture

c. Client's typical response to change(s) imposed by outer conditions or others
d. Client's typical way of handling self-chosen change(s)
e. Stress-reduction strategies used by client (ask specifically about drugs and alcohol)
f. Usual management of anxiety and fear (ask about drugs and alcohol specifically)
g. Usual way of dealing with anger (range from irritation to fury)
h. Awareness of any chronic illnesses that are particularly sensitive to stress

Establishing the Climate of Acceptance

Whether working with clients individually, in pairs, or in family groups I recommend you begin by helping them to identify and work through – and heal – the places in their relationships that block certain qualities of the climate of acceptance. Simultaneously, it will be helpful to assist them to strengthen the qualities in their relationships that promote the climate of acceptance. You serve as healer and facilitator in the creation, strengthening, and maintaining of the climate. It has the following qualities: a) nurturing, b) valuing, c) forgiving, d) sharing, e) caring, f) compassion, g) laughing, and h) renewing or rejuvenating relationships. As you undertake your pivotal role in the establishment of such a climate, it will be helpful to keep in mind the basic assumptions underlying the adult-to-adult model.

Carl Rogers' concept of unconditional positive regard is often misconstrued as a blanket approval of any behavior, regardless of its consequences or

merits. You will need to help your clients understand that the concept refers to a quality much
deeper than opinion or approval of behavior. The
terminology "unconditional" refers to being
nonjudgmental of the person, the true core of the
individual. Help your clients differentiate between
accepting the person and condoning or approving
behavior.

The ability to distinguish between love of the
person and approval of the person's behavior is
integral to establishing and maintaining a climate
of acceptance. The exchanges of goals, hopes,
aspirations, unfinished business, and other topics
pertinent to working with the model require authenticity. Your clients cannot make authentic
disclosures unless they feel safe. For example,
parent/child dyads often have long-standing issues
of lack of understanding or judging the other's
behavior.

Every aspect of this model is embedded in the
climate of acceptance. None of the changing, learning, risk-taking, or problem-solving should be undertaken out of the context of developing and
cultivating the climate of acceptance. The work
undertaken in the journey is difficult within the
most ideal of climates. In anything less than an
accepting, compassionate climate it can be brutal.
Establishing the necessary climate is the underpinning of therapeutic use of the model.

Teaching and Applying the *RISC* Strategy

Taking well-considered risks offers the prospect of stronger, more enjoyable, and healthier
relationships. However, keep in mind that taking

risks might uncover or even introduce new problems in relationships. Encourage your clients to approach risk-taking with preparation and careful consideration. Remind them that an emotional risk does not take place in just one moment. It may feel like the equivalent of jumping off a cliff, but it should not actually be that precipitous. Altering a situation by taking a risk requires time. It is helpful to keep in mind that relationships do not develop in a moment and will not change in a moment.

Help your clients formulate their ideas about what they want. Encourage them to set their own pace. When you recognize resistance is interfering with their ability to proceed, confront the resistance and deal with it in psychotherapy. I recommend you introduce your clients to David Viscott's book, Risking, or a reference you prefer to help them learn healthy attitudes toward risking. Consider introducing Sam Keen's recent book, Learning to Fly, for clients you believe can profit from his wisdom about overcoming fears. Obviously, if you recommend readings to your clients, the choice entails your assessing whether they have the reading skills to comprehend and assimilate the material.

Teach your clients the four steps involved in the *RISC* strategy as they are discussed in the Introduction and Overview of the book. Explain that the strategy will be used over and over with a variety of applications as they work through the model. Help them understand that each time they reach an awareness about something in their relationships and the quality of their lives that they want to change toward improved health, that awareness is the beginning of Recognition. Another cycle of *RISC* begins with that Recognition. As you listen to your clients, be alert for opportunities to guide them to apply *RISC* to the psychological work they are doing. Here are some points to emphasize as you teach your clients the steps involved in *RISC*:

1. Recognizing: The initial step begins with awareness of the need to change. Help your clients verbalize and summarize what they Recognize. Recognition often involves owning discomfort with some specific interactions in relationships. For example, a client said to me, "I don't know what's wrong; but I know I want to figure out a way to talk to him without both of us getting mad." Another common experience involves dissatisfaction with emotional overtones of a relationship, e.g. a daughter who experienced free-floating anxiety when she and her mother were together despite the surface appearance that they were comfortable in each other's presence. In some instances, adults perceive their relationship as satisfactory or even excellent, but one or both of them recognizes it is 'shadowed' by dread of what the future may bring into their relationship. An example of the latter is wives who are aware of a dread or a fear of outliving their husbands.

2. Inventorying: Topics for this step are derived from the Recognition step. Once your clients have a clear statement of what they Recognize they want or need to change, direct them to begin their Inventory. Clients are sometimes too overwhelmed with the complexity of what they have Recognized to begin their Inventory right away. As their therapist, you will judge when they can begin their Inventory. Generally, the sooner they begin, with your guidance, the less overwhelmed they will continue to feel.

The Inventory should be in writing. It is best if your clients write it while they discuss it with you. Nevertheless, you may ascertain that your client needs you to do the writing. Insist clients begin their Inventory with strengths although it will include problems as well. Actively involve yourself in helping them identify available resources to add to the list of strengths.

Clients, particularly if they are depressed, may declare they cannot list strengths because they perceive none. In such instances, help them understand that being present and beginning an effort to improve their lives is, in itself, a strength. If you encounter a client who actually cannot continue working through *RISC* at a given time, re-evaluate your assessment of the person's ego strength and proceed with therapy as indicated. Re-introduce *RISC* when your client becomes healthier.

3. Structuring: This step may begin as soon as the participants are able to formulate a plan for how they will build on their strengths to change their relationships. The time it takes to reach this point in the strategy varies not only with individuals but also with each time *RISC* is used. This is the step in which the goals for desired change that were Recognized are actualized. In this step, the structure of the relationship is changed intentionally. Help your clients understand that Structuring will remain a life-long challenge, because healthy relationships and healthy lives involve growth, learning, and taking the journey into aging in the spirit of shared adventure. One of the most helpful aspects of including Structuring as a specific step is that, by doing so, you reinforce your clients' confidence that they can be proactive in their lives. With respect for their differences and the variables in relationships, all clients are guided when they are Structuring their relationships to do at least the following:

a. Plan how they will build on their strengths
b. Agree on how they want their relationship to function
c. Decide what their 'building materials' will be – journals, study, workshops, counseling, prayer, body work, therapy, retreats, other
d. Spend scheduled time on strategies to improve communication, as well as using those strategies in their everyday interactions with one another
e. Plan periods of rest from the work to have fun together
f. Be authentic, clear, and compassionate with one another
g. Remain mindful of the importance of doing everything in a climate of acceptance
h. Recognize when one or both of them need help and be willing to ask for help.

4. Choosing: This fourth step is included to guide participants in focusing on specific choices about how they will continue to structure their relationships and accomplish their goals. Review with clients who have learned the basics of applying *RISC* and been introduced to the model that they are making the following choices:

a. to be partners in the journey of aging
b. to be pioneers in relating to one another adult-to-adult
c. to remain committed throughout to a compassionate journey
d. to explore and to change as they grow
e. to respect each other's differences
f. to support, nurture, and forgive one another
g. to face the end of the journey together

Examples of the choices clients most frequently choose to make include:

a. living arrangements
b. management of finances
c. resolving long-standing family conflicts
d. disagreements about handling grandchildren
e. becoming more <u>inter</u>dependent
f. handling arguments and even minor disagreements
g. understanding each other's values and spiritual beliefs
h. advanced directives and funeral plans
i. disposition of family heirlooms and items of sentimental value
j. concern about health issues that may interfere with their relationship
k. disagreements about habits, e.g., smoking
l. changing habitual communication patterns that are outmoded
m. grieving and losses
n. ways to respond to the continual challenge to keep their hearts open to one another, be forgiving, and deal with one another compassionately

Working through the Elements Sequentially

Relating Adult to Adult

You and your clients need a common reference point for beginning to work through the elements. If your clients began their journey with the workshop, "Aging as a Shared Journey," they will have completed Form 1 in Chapter 1. Ask them to share their answers with you. If they did not attend the workshop, have them complete the two sentences from Form 1, Chapter 1 before you begin to coach them through the territory of adult-to-adult relating to each other. Use their answers as the place to begin. Typically, there will be congruence between the answers they gave on Form 1 and the problems they identified in **Recognizing** when they were learning to use *RISC*. If, on the other hand, the two contain highly dissimilar responses, choose to begin with the problem that seems most acute.

Using the problem you and your clients have identified and described in writing, utilize the exercises recommended in the book along with 'favorites' of yours to accomplish the following:

Through the use of *RISC*; communication exercises, relaxation exercises, role-play, and other experiential learning exercises, teach clients the basics of relating as adult-to-adult by:
  a. demonstrating respect for their differences
  b. negotiating as equals while mindful of the nature of their relationship
  c. learning new ways to talk, work, and play together
  d. allowing space for growth both separately and together
  e. moving their relationship balance of dependence/

independence toward interdependence.

Note: You should remain alert for opportunities to reinforce the importance of doing their heartwork and of working through the model within the context of a climate of acceptance at all times. These two foundational concepts must become integrated into the fabric of their lives.

Meeting the Challenges of Aging and Illness

Review the challenges listed in Chapter 3. List the specific challenges you and your clients identify, e.g., increasing frailty of the elder. Focus on each challenge listed as you apply *RISC* to your work with each challenge. For example, if your clients identify the increasing frailty of the elder, you would guide them to Inventory their strengths and resources and problems associated with that frailty.

Continue to work through the steps of *RISC* with respect to that challenge before proceeding to another. Keep in mind that fear of aging is often one of the challenges your clients need to Recognize. In addition, be aware that as you begin to work with the challenges, additional ones may emerge. Proceeding at the pace appropriate for your clients, guide them through each challenge listed by helping them explore the following:
   a. decisions about health they currently face as well as those they anticipate
   b. feelings about financial and legal concerns (refer to legal and financial resource persons when clients need advice in those areas)
   c. independence/dependence issues
   d. decisions about how and where to live

   e. changes in parent/child relationships as both age
   f. taking risks
   g. remaining active – physically; mentally; spiritually
   h. making new friends – losing old ones and grieving losses
   i. aging together by growing together as one adult to another

Communicating Clearly and Compassionately

   Supervise your clients' efforts to learn more effective communication as described in Chapter 4. If you are applying the model to your work with a number of clients, I recommend you use the group format to teach communication and relaxation exercises. Having taught them the basics, you can then facilitate your clients' use of what they learned to focus on their specific issues. Keep in mind the concept of communication being a thread that is woven throughout the whole of the model. Remain alert for opportunities to teach improved communication with any aspect of the model your clients are learning.

   Be creative in ways you and your clients work together to develop communication that embraces the following qualities, being mindful that they are of equal importance. Help your clients understand the nuances of meaning of the terms in the qualities listed below:
   a. compassion
   b. patience
   c. authenticity
   d. respect
   e. nurturing

f.   valuing
g.   gentleness
h.   forgiveness
i.   loving humor

Resolving Unfinished Business

Learning to relate to one another as adult-to-adult involves dealing with minor unfinished business as well as major life concerns we usually associate with death and dying. Refer to communication exercises in Chapter 2 and to suggestions in Chapter 4 to help your clients with this element. Coach your clients in individual and paired exercises to help them deal with questions related to unfinished business such as:

a.   What do you wish you could tell the other?
b.   What feels too 'petty' to bring up?
c.   What do you need to explain?
d.   What do you need to know about the other?
e.   What do you need the other to know about you?
f.   Where in your life do you need comfort?
g.   What do you need to forgive/have forgiven?
h.   What do you need to feel safe to deal with the issues above?

Remain alert for opportunities to help your clients understand how energy that is freed by releasing and resolving unfinished business can contribute to energizing them for more vital living.

Facing the End of the Journey

You and your clients may want to review Chapter 6 together as you begin working with this element. Encourage your clients to explore their feelings about dealing with the inevitability that the 'end' of their journey together will be death. Provide emotional support as needed during such exploration. Respect for individual spiritual beliefs is particularly important in dealing with this element. Death may or may not be viewed by your clients as an 'end.' It is characterized for the purposes of this model as the end of the journey the participants mutually agreed to undertake as an adventure into aging together. Be especially aware of the following important facets of facing the end – all are important. The list is not prioritized.

   a. religious and spiritual beliefs and preferences
   b. cultural beliefs and preferences about death and dying
   c. family beliefs and preferences about death and dying
   d. idiosyncratic beliefs and preferences about death and dying

   Help your clients explore, preferably together with their fellow traveler(s), such topics as:
   a. attending to practical aspects, e.g., making a will and executing advanced directives
   b. opening their hearts to one another about their fears of dying and death
   c. making and discussing plans for funerals, memorials, and related topics
   d. assisting one another in the grieving process
   e. being actively involved in living until death

Frequently Asked Questions about Using "Aging as a Shared Journey" as a Clinical Intervention

   1. What if my assessment indicates one member

of a dyad is an appropriate candidate for the model, but the other is not?

Answer: Use your clinical judgment to decide, as you would with any therapeutic treatment plan. Some choices that I have found useful are:

a. Let the pair try the intervention and reality-test your impressions. You may be surprised at what they can handle. Or, they may learn by recognizing it themselves that they are not ready or not well suited to the intervention.

b. Work unilaterally with the one who is ready, encouraging his/her practice with a willing adult who is not the adult for whom the work is inappropriate.

c. Treat the client who is not an appropriate candidate as you would in your regular practice. Consider the model again when that client improves.

d. Evaluate precisely what aspects of the model you assess the client as unable to handle. Consider whether there is a workable modification of that aspect that does not violate the integrity of the model. For example, if the client cannot tolerate overt anger, such tools as journals, controlled exercises, or other strategies may be used.

e. Compare the approach you would typically use with that client to the approach you would use with the model. Ask yourself whether the difference is substantial. If not, try using the model on a limited basis with one specific, identified challenge of aging. Keep in mind that using the model does not negate your use of additional clinical inter-

ventions to which you are more accustomed –
unless authoritarian orders are in your reper-
toire. If they are, why are you reading this book?

2. What kinds of reactions might I expect from
my clients when teaching them about the climate of acceptance?

Answer: When the content of the work is relatively non-threatening to your clients, they will
probably find developing the climate of acceptance rewarding. It is not unusual for clients to
express relief at their realization that the qualities of the climate of acceptance are much of
what they have been needing in their lives generally.
Some additional reactions I have encountered are:

a. When the content of the work threatens the
    clients' defenses, their concept of themselves,
    or their world views, they will resort to old
    patterns of blaming, rejecting, judging, and
    demanding that threaten the very core of the
    climate of acceptance. At such times, your
    role in assisting them to re-establish, culti-
    vate, nourish, and maintain the climate of
    acceptance will be pivotal to their ability to
    continue to do the work this model entails.
b. Clients sometimes need a lot of encourage-
    ment to trust the process. The work can be
    difficult, anxiety-producing, and threatening.
    You need to encourage your clients to trust
    your expertise. Qualities such as joy and
    confidence result from mastery of continuing
    to grow as the journey continues, and those
    qualities can only grow in 'soil' nourished by
    the climate of acceptance. You can help your
    clients understand the relationship between the

work of changing and the benefits that can result.

c. Your evaluation, your clients' feedback, or both, may indicate that certain clients have worked so intensely that a time-out is advisable. Situations may occur that necessitate an agreement to interrupt the work specifically associated with difficult aspects of the journey. For example, clients sometimes show an initial burst of energy and excitement about their potential for change and make too many changes too fast. If that happens, provide them with guidance about whether to cease altogether (rarely necessary) or how to handle a time-out.

d. Clients may decide it is time to stop working with you prematurely in the process. Use your therapist's knowledge concerning resistance and blocking to help them decide whether to continue, take a time-out, or discontinue. If you are out of contact with clients who began the process and stopped for six weeks or longer, I advise that you review the model with them and reassess their willingness and ability to go further.

3. What are the kinds of information about the clients' cultural backgrounds that I need to know?

Answer: Your cultural background data on your clients should include but not be limited to:

a. Culture of origin vs. culture of present habitation

b. Extent to which clients' families maintained cultural values and practices, e.g., speaking the native language in the home and English as a second language

c. Health care practices in the culture of origin

and who are the respected health care practitioners in the culture of origin

d. Traditions, concepts of illness, perceptions of life and death, folk medicine practices, and any available ethnic information about your clients and their families and home environments

4. Does the author arrange workshops and provide consultation in the use of the model if requested?

Answer: I welcome your contacts to discuss your requests and learn whether they can be met through EDUPLACE, my consultation and educational business. Dissemination of "Aging as a Shared Journey" as a model for healthy aging is the major activity of EDUPLACE. Workshops, consultations, and exchange of information are the major avenues of extending the model. I also welcome your sharing your experiences in using the model, in the spirit of a mutual climate of acceptance. Contact me at:

1-785-840-0358

or

eduplace@cjnetworks.com

Thank you for reading the book and considering the model as an addition to your clinical interventions. I wish you the best for rewarding experiences with its use. Welcome to the growing ranks of pioneers who are committed to healthy aging for themselves, their clients, and their loved ones.

References

Introduction and Overview

Butler, R. N. (1975). *Why survive? Being old in America.* NY: Harper & Row.

Butler, R.N., Lewis, M., & Sunderland, T. (1991). *Aging and mental health*, 4th ed. NY: Macmillan Publishing Co.

Delany, S., Delany, E. & Hearth, A.H. (1993). *Having our say: The Delany sisters' first 100 years.* NY: Kodansha America, Inc.

Delany, S. (1995). *On my own.* NY: Kodansha America, Inc.

Dychtwald, K. & Flower, J. (1990). *Age wave: How the most important trend of our time will change your future.* NY: Bantam Books.

Friedan, B. (1993). *The fountain of age.* NY: Simon & Schuster.

Pegels, C.C. (1988). *Health care and the older citizen: Economic, demographic, and financial aspects.* Rockville, MD: Aspen Publishers, Inc.

Rogers, C.R. (1961). *On becoming a person.* Boston: Houghton Mifflin.

Chapter 1: Heartwork

Blattner, B. (1981). *Holistic nursing.* Englewood Cliffs, NJ: Prentice-Hall, Inc.

Erikson, E.H., Erikson, J.M., & Kivnick, H.Q. (1986). *Vital involvement in old age: The experience of old age in our time.* NY: W.W. Norton & Company.

Kabat-zinn, J. (1994). *Wherever you go there you are: Mindfulness meditation in everyday life.* NY: Hyperion.

Lazarus, A. (1984). *In the mind's eye: The power of imagery for personal enrichment.* NY: The Guilford Press.

Pipher, M. (1999). *Another country: Navigating the emotional terrain of our elders.* NY: Riverhead Books/Penquin Putnam, Inc.

Powell, J. (1969). *Why am I afraid to tell you who I am?* Chicago: Peacock Books.

Williams, M. (1975). *The velveteen rabbit: Or how to become real.* NY: Avon Books.

Chapter 2: Relating Adult to Adult

Carter, B. & McGoldrick, M., Eds. (1988). *The changing family life cycle: A framework for family therapy,* 2nd ed. NY: Gardner Press.

Palmore, E.B. (1990). *Ageism: Negative and positive.* NY: Springer Publishing Co.

Perlmutter, M. & Hall, E. (1992). *Adult development and aging,* 2nd ed. NY: John Wiley & Sons, Inc.

Peterson, C., Maier, S.F., Seligman, M.E.P (1995). *Learned helplessnes: A theory for the age of personal control.* NY: Oxford.

Viscott, D. (1977). *Risking.* NY: Pocket Books.

Chapter 3: Meeting the Challenges of Illness & Aging: Learning to Use *RISC*

Anderson-Ellis, E (1993). *Aging parents & you: A complete handbook to help you help your elders maintain a healthy, productive and independent life.* NY: MasterMedia Ltd.

Bandura, A. (1977). *Self-efficacy: Toward a unifying theory of behavioral change.* Psychological Review, 84, 191-215.

Bandura, A. (1981). "Self-referent thought: A developmental analysis of self-efficacy." In J.H. Flavell & L.D. Ross (Eds.), *Cognitive social development: Frontiers and possible futures.* NY: Cambridge University Press.

Benson, H. & Klipper, M.Z. (1976). *The relaxation response.* NY: William Morrow & Company, Inc.

Bridges, W. (1980). *Transitions: Making sense of life's changes.* Reading, MA: Addison-Wesley Publishing Co.

Butler, R.N., Lewis, M., & Sunderland, T. (1991). *Aging and mental health,* 4th ed. NY: McMillan Publishing Co.

Carlsen, M.B. (1988). *Meaning-making: Therapeutic processes in adult development.* NY: W.W. Norton & Co.

Cousins, N. (1979). *Anatomy of an illness.* NY: W. W. Norton & Co.

Dychtwald, K. & Flower, J. (1990). *Age wave: How the most important trend of our time will change your future.* NY: Bantam Books.

Ebersole, P. & Hess, P. (1989). *Toward healthy aging: Human needs and nursing response,* 3rd ed. St. Louis: The C.V. Mosby Co.

Gubrium, J.F. (1993). *Speaking of life: Horizons of meaning for nursing home residents.* NY: Aldine De Gruyter.

Lazarus, A. (1977). *In the mind's eye: The power of imagery for personal enrichment.* NY: The Guilford Press.

Luce, G.G. (1992). *Longer life, more joy: Techniques for enhancing health, happiness, and inner vision.* North Hollywood, CA: Newcastle Publishing Co., Inc.

Peterson, C. & Bossio, L.M. (1991). *Health and optimism.* NY: The Free Press.

Peterson, C., Meier, S.F., & Seligman, M.E.P. (1995). *Learned helplessness: A theory for the age of_personal control.* NY: Oxford.

Seligman, M.E.P. (1998). *Learned optimism.* NY: Pocket Books.

Chapter 4: Communicating Clearly & Compassionately

Bandler, R. & Grinder, J. (1975). *The structure of magic, Vol. I and II.* Palo Alto, CA: Science and Behavior Books, Inc.

Bandler, R. & Grinder, J. (1979). *Frogs into princes: Neuro linguistic programming.* Moab, Utah: Real People Press.

Benson, H. & Klipper, M. (1976). *The relaxation response.* NY: William Morrow and Co., Inc.

Blattner, B. (1981). *Holistic Nursing.* Englewood Cliffs, NJ: Prentice-Hall, Inc.

Cameron, J. (1992). *The artist's way: A spiritual path to higher creativity.* NY: A Jeremy P. Tarcher/Putnam Book.

Covey, S., Merrill, A. R., & Merrill, R. R. (1994). *First things first.* NY: Simon & Schuster.

Girdano, D. & Everly, G. (1979). *Controlling stress & tension: A holistic approach.* Englewood Cliffs, NJ: Prentice-Hall, Inc.

Goleman, D. (1995). *Emotional intelligence.* NY: Bantam Books.

Houston, J. (1982). *The possible human: A course in enhancing your physical, mental, and creative abilities.* Los Angeles, CA: J.B. Tarcher, Inc.

Lazarus, A. (1977). *In the mind's eye: The power of imagery for personal enrichment.* NY: The Guilford Press.

Luce, G.G. (1992). *Longer life, more joy: Techniques for enhancing health, happiness, and inner vision.* North Hollywood, CA: Newcastle Publishing Co., Inc.

Shapiro Jr., D. H. (1980). *Meditation: Self-regulation strategy and altered state of consciousness.* NY: Aldine Publishing Co.

Tannen, D. (1990). *You just don't understand: Women and men in conversation.* NY: Ballentine Books.

Woolfolk, R. L. & Lehrer, P.M. (1984). *Principles and practice of stress management.* NY: The Guilford Press.

Chapter 5: Resolving Unfinished Business

Bloom-Feshbach, J., Bloom-Feshbach, S., & Associates. (1987). *The psychology of separation and loss.* San Francisco: Jossey-Bass Publishers.

Callanan, M. & Kelley, P. (1993). "Needing Reconciliation." *In Final gifts: Understanding the special awareness, needs, and communications of the dying.* NY: Bantam Books

Hargrave, T.D. (1994). *Families and forgiveness: Healing wounds in the intergenerational family.* NY: Bruner/Mazel Publishers.

Levine, S. (1984). *Meetings at the edge: Dialogues with the grieving and the dying, the healing and the healed.* Garden City, NY: Anchor Press.

Moody, Jr., R.A. (1975). *Life after life: The investigation of a phenomenon – survival of bodily death.* Covington, GA: Mockingbird Books, Inc.

Chapter 6: Facing the End of the Journey

Albom, M. (1997). *Tuesdays with Morrie.* NY: Doubleday.

Callanan, M. & Kelly, P. (1993). *Final gifts: Understanding the special awareness, needs, and communications of the dying.* NY: Bantam Books.

Frankl, V.E. (1964). *Man's search for meaning: An introduction to Logotherapy.* NY: Washing Square Press, Inc.

Kubler-Ross, E. (1974). *On death and dying.* NY: Macmillan Publishing Co., Inc.

Kubler-Ross, E. (1975). *Death: The final stage of growth.* Englewood Cliffs, NJ: Prentice-Hall, Inc.

Kubler-Ross, E. (1978). *To live until we say good-bye.* Englewood Cliffs, NJ: Prentice-Hall, Inc.

Levine, S. (1982). *Who dies? An investigation of conscious living and conscious dying.* Garden City, NY: Anchor Press.

Lucas, M. (1999). "Recognizing and resolving 'unfinished business': Coping with terminal illness and dying." *The Kansas Nurse,* 74 (10), 6-8.

Nouwen, H.J. (1994). *Our greatest gift: A meditation on dying and caring.* San Francisco, CA: Harper San Francisco.

Appendix for Mental Health Professionals

Brigham, D.D. (1994). *Imagery for getting well: Clinical applications of behavioral medicine.* NY: W.W. Norton & Company, Inc.

Brody, C.M. & Semel, V.G. (1993). *Strategies for therapy with the elderly: Living with hope and meaning.* NY: Springer Publishing Co.

Budman, S.H. & Gurman, A.S. (1988). *Theory and practice of brief therapy.* NY: The Guilford Press.

Butler, R.N., Lewis, M., & Sunderland, T. (1991). *Aging and mental health,* 4th ed. NY: Macmillan Publishing Co.

Carlsen, M.B. (1988). *Meaning-making: Therapeutic processes in adult development.* NY: W. W. Norton & Co.

"Diagnosis and treatment of depression in late life." (1991). Reprinted from *NIH Consensus Development Conference Consensus Statement 1991* Nov. 4-6: 9(3), Bethesda, MD: National Institutes of Health.

Dobson, K.S. (Ed.). (1988). *Handbook of cognitive-behavioral therapies.* NY: The Guilford Press.

Ebersole, P. & Hess, P. (1990). *Toward healthy aging: Human needs and nursing response,* 3rd ed. St. Louis: The C.V. Mosby Co.

Erikson, E.H., Erikson, J.M., & Kivnick, H.Q. (1986). *Vital involvement in old age: The experience of old age in our time.* NY: W.W. Norton & Co.

Genevay, B. & Katz, R.S. (Eds.) (1990). *Countertransference and older clients.* Newbury Park: Sage Publications.

Keen, S. (1999). *Learning to fly.* NY: Broadway Books/Random House, Inc.

Lazarus, R.S. & Folkman, S. (1984). *Stress, appraisal, and coping.* NY: Springer Publishing Co.

Lucas, M. (1999). "Recognizing and resolving 'unfinished business': Coping with terminal illness and dying." *The Kansas Nurse.* Vol. 74, No.10, 6-8.

Meyers, W. (Ed.). (1991). *New techniques in the psychotherapy of older patients.* Washington, DC: American Psychiatric Press, Inc.

Salzman, C. (1990). *Principles of psychopharmacology.* In D. Biennenfeld (Ed.).

Verwoedt's clinical geropsychiatry, 3rd ed. Baltimore: Williams & Wilkens.

Salkovskis, P.M. (Ed.) (1996). *Frontiers of cognitive therapy.* NY: The Guilford Press.

Viscott, D. (1977). *Risking.* NY: Pocket Books.

Additional Suggested Readings for Healthy Living

Borysenko, J. (1994). *Fire in the soul: A new psychology of spiritual optimism.* NY: Warner Books, Inc.

Breathnach, S.B. (1995). *Simple abundance: A daybook of comfort and joy.* NY: Warner Books, Inc.

Breathnach, S.F. (1998). *Something more: Excavating your authentic self.* NY: Warner Books, Inc.

Cameron, J. (1996). *The vein of gold: A journey to your creative heart.* NY: Jeremy P. Tarcher/ Putnam

Dyer, W.W. (1980). *The sky's the limit.* NY: Simon and Schuster.

Elliott, W. (1996). *Tying rocks to clouds: Meetings and conversations with wise and spiritual people.* NY: Image Books Doubleday.

Hillman, J. (1999). *The force of character and the lasting life.* NY: Random House.

Kollock, P. & O'Brien, J. (1994). *The production of reality: Essays and readings in social psychology.* Thousand Oaks, CA: Pine Forge Press.

Moore, T. (1996). *The education of the heart.* NY: HarperCollins Publishers, Inc.

Moore, T. (1996). *The re-enchantment of every-day life.* NY: HarperCollins Publishers, Inc.

Prather, H. (1977). *Notes on love and courage.* Garden City, NY: Doubleday & Co., Inc.

Wellwood, J. (Ed). (1992). *Ordinary magic: Everyday life as spiritual path.* Boston & London: Shambhala.

Whitmyer, C. (Ed). (1993). *In the company of others: Making community in the Modern World.* NY: Jeremy P. Tarcher/Perigree Books

Index

A

abandonment 173
acceptance
> 34, 37, 41, 53, 54, 55, 57, 58, 68, 69, 70, 71, 74, 75, 86, 92, 95, 125, 128, 129, 130, 132, 162, 166, 167, 180, 194, 199, 200, 201, 212, 218, 221, 223, 224, 227, 228, 232, 235, 240, 242

adult-to-adult
> 25, 27, 33, 38, 67, 70, 73, 75, 77, 84, 86, 94, 95, 99, 105, 106, 124, 131, 132, 133, 140, 153, 194, 222, 227, 233, 234, 237

age wave 24
ageism 24, 84, 85, 102
aging well 27, 30, 37, 39, 40, 67, 100, 128
anger 15, 28, 58, 62, 78, 134, 135, 136, 140, 145, 146, 147, 164, 166, 198, 199, 201, 225, 227, 239
Annabel and Mack 75, 163, 165, 166, 167
Autonomy vs. Shame and Doubt 31

B

baby boomer 23, 25, 26, 51, 127, 218
balanced perspective 23, 25, 128
basic assumptions 29, 30, 227
Basic Trust vs. Basic Mistrust 31
Beren 208, 209

C

caregiver 33, 99, 105, 106, 107, 109, 110, 221
case manager 108
Catherine and Helen 169, 170, 171, 172, 173
change
> 8, 13, 16, 26, 27, 28, 30, 33, 34, 37, 39, 44, 49, 50, 52, 53, 57, 58, 59, 60, 62, 63, 67, 73, 75, 80, 81, 82, 83, 84, 86, 111, 120, 121, 122, 123, 124, 126, 130, 139, 144, 149, 152, 159, 175, 219, 220, 225, 227, 229, 230, 233, 236, 241

choosing
> 27, 29, 36, 50, 81, 86, 92, 93, 94, 97, 114, 115, 129, 148, 151, 152, 175, 232

climate of acceptance
> 34, 37, 53, 54, 55, 57, 68, 69, 70, 71, 75, 86, 92, 95, 125, 128, 129, 130, 132, 166, 194, 212, 218, 221, 223, 224, 227, 228, 232, 235, 240, 242

cognitive restructuring 129, 139, 225
communication exercise 36, 77, 153, 155, 158, 160, 234, 237
compassion
      35, 37, 41, 54, 57, 58, 63, 64, 75, 91, 92, 95, 104, 114, 127, 131,
          132, 133, 135, 137, 138, 140, 144, 145, 146, 147, 148, 149, 152,
          155, 160, 180, 194, 210, 223, 227, 228, 232, 233, 236, 249
compassionate communication 144, 147, 148, 149, 155

D

death
      9, 19, 20, 31, 37, 38, 39, 43, 46, 49, 62, 95, 106, 107, 119, 123,
          126, 128, 162, 176, 177, 179, 180, 182, 185, 186, 187, 188, 189, 190,
          191, 193, 194, 195, 199, 200, 204, 205, 206, 208, 209, 210,
          211, 214, 221, 237, 238, 242, 251
denial 99, 110, 129, 186, 188, 190, 199, 201, 209, 211
depression
      45, 87, 93, 103, 111, 116, 117, 118, 119, 124, 146, 171, 172, 173, 199,
          201, 224, 252
Dianne and Tony 199, 200, 201
disability
      30, 62, 99, 100, 101, 103, 104, 105, 106, 109, 112, 116, 120,
          123, 126, 127, 128, 129, 220
dying
      37, 38, 95, 123, 124, 127, 141, 159, 162, 186, 187, 188, 189, 190,
          191, 195, 196, 198, 199, 200, 205, 206, 207, 209, 210, 211, 212,
          237, 238, 250, 251, 252, 253

E

Ed 83, 84, 85, 86, 92, 115, 118
effective communication
      33, 131, 132, 134, 137, 139, 149, 182, 236
Ego Integrity vs. Despair 221
Emily and Ruth 78, 79, 80, 110, 150, 151

F

family myths & secrets 168
forgiveness 37, 161, 162, 167, 168, 203, 237, 251

G

Generativity vs. Stagnation 31, 32, 221
geriatric clinics 101
geropsychiatric 46
grief 42, 111, 181, 182, 200, 210, 211

grieving 37, 39, 43, 95, 111, 147, 187, 211, 233, 236, 238, 251
guided imagery 113, 114, 137, 174

H

heartwork
    34, 40, 41, 43, 55, 57, 58, 65, 68, 69, 153, 221, 235, 246
holistic 8, 88, 116, 117, 129, 145, 246, 249

I

Identity vs. Confusion 31
imagery 55, 113, 114, 137, 174, 246, 248, 250, 252
Industry vs. Inferiority 31
infantalizing 106, 115
Initiative vs. Guilt 31
Integrity vs. Despair 31, 32, 57, 221
interdependence 36, 72, 235
intergenerational 8, 9, 27, 129, 221, 251
Intimacy vs. Isolation 31
inventorying
    27, 36, 50, 81, 86, 88, 91, 97, 110, 111, 112, 125, 148, 149, 199, 230

J

Jane 141
Jim 146, 147

L

learned helplessness 85, 124, 125, 249
life moment 173, 176, 180
Lionel Sr. and Lionel Jr. 201, 202, 203, 204, 205

M

Margaret 86, 87
Mary and Jill 176, 177, 178, 179, 180, 181
meaning
    19, 34, 35, 45, 51, 64, 72, 85, 88, 101, 105, 123, 124, 130, 140,
        141, 156, 179, 180, 195, 196, 201, 214, 222, 236, 248, 251, 252
meaning-making 34, 35, 124, 130, 222, 248, 252
methodology 25, 31

N

Nancy and Doug 206, 207
near-death experience 177, 179

O

optimism 100, 190, 248, 249, 254

P

pathfinder 161, 183
pioneer 8, 20, 28, 29, 31, 39, 45, 92, 95, 153, 220, 233, 242
psychotherapy 35, 50, 117, 118, 139, 162, 195, 219, 226, 229, 253

R

Ralph 42, 43, 181, 182, 183
recognizing
    27, 36, 50, 54, 61, 63, 80, 81, 82, 86, 87, 88, 96, 110, 140,
    159, 163, 230, 234, 252, 253
relaxation response 114, 137, 207, 247, 249
reminiscence 83, 92, 141, 172
RISC
    27, 28, 35, 36, 50, 67, 73, 80, 81, 86, 89, 91, 92, 96, 99, 104, 109, 110,
    111, 114, 117, 118, 131, 132, 140, 148, 188, 205, 219, 223, 224, 225,
    228, 229, 230, 231, 232, 234, 235, 247
risking 58, 68, 229
role-play 36, 69, 125, 234

S

self-efficacy 100, 247
self-in-becoming 113, 114
spirituality 64, 112, 167, 172
stardust companions 11, 14, 15, 16, 160
stress reduction 36, 114, 137, 138, 174
structuring
    27, 36, 50, 81, 86, 89, 90, 91, 92, 93, 97, 110, 113, 128, 139, 148,
    149, 203, 232
Sylvia 88, 89, 104
synchronicity 158
synchronized breathing 206, 207

U

unconditional positive regard 34, 57, 167, 227
unfinished business
    21, 35, 38, 59, 94, 157, 158, 159, 161, 162, 163, 166, 167,
    169, 172, 173, 174, 175, 176, 180, 182, 183, 187, 194, 212,
    224, 228, 237, 250, 252, 253

V

vignettes. *See* Annabel and Mack; Beren; Catherine and
Helen; Dianne and Tony; Ed; Emily and
Ruth; Jane; Jim; Lionel Sr. and Lionel Jr.; Margaret; Mary and
Jill; Nancy and Doug; Ralph; Sylvia; Vivian and
Howard; Walter and Eloise
Vivian and Howard 46, 47, 48, 50, 52, 53, 54, 55, 56, 57, 59, 110

W

Walter and Eloise 125, 128, 129